British History in Persp(
General Editor: Jeremy 1

PUBLISHED TITLES

Titles continued overleaf

List continued from previous page

Bruce Webster *Medieval Scotland*
Ann Williams *Kingship and Government in Pre-Conquest England*
John W. Young *Britain and European Unity, 1945–92*
Michael B. Young *Charles I*

FORTHCOMING

Walter L. Arnstein *Queen Victoria*
Ian Arthurson *Henry VII*
Toby Barnard *The Kingdom of Ireland, 1640–1740*
Eugenio Biagini *Gladstone*
Peter Catterall *The Labour Party, 1918–1945*
Gregory Claeys *The French Revolution Debate in Britain*
Pauline Croft *James I*
Eveline Cruickshanks *The Glorious Revolution*
John Davis *British Politics, 1885–1939*
David Dean *Parliament and Politics in Elizabethan and Jacobean England,
1558–1614*
Colin Eldridge *The Victorians Overseas*
Richard English *The IRA*
Alan Heesom *The Anglo-Irish Union, 1800–1922*
I. G. C. Hutchison *Scottish Politics in the Twentieth Century*
Gareth Jones *Wales, 1700–1980: Crisis of Identity*
H. S. Jones *Political Thought in Nineteenth-Century Britain*
D. E. Kennedy *The English Revolution, 1642–1649*
Carol Levin *The Reign of Elizabeth I*
Roger Mason *Kingship and Tyranny? Scotland, 1513–1603*
Hiram Morgan *Ireland in the Early Modern Periphery, 1534–1690*
R. C. Nash *English Foreign Trade and the World Economy, 1600–1800*
Robin Prior and Trevor Wilson *Britain and the Impact of World War I*
Brian Quintrell *Government and Politics in Early Stuart England*
Stephen Roberts *Governance in England and Wales, 1603–1688*
David Scott *The British Civil Wars*
Alan Sykes *The Radical Right in Britain*
Ann Wiekel *The Elizabethan Counter-Revolution*
Ian Wood *Churchill*

Please note that a sister series, *Social History in Perspective*, is now available.
It covers the key topics in social, cultural and religious history.

British History in Perspective
Series Standing Order
ISBN 0–333–71356–7 hardcover
ISBN 0–333–69331–0 paperback
(*outside North America only*)

You can receive future titles in this series as they are published by placing a
standing order. Please contact your bookseller or, in case of difficulty, write to us
at the address below with your name and address, the title of the series and the
ISBN quoted above.

Customer Services Department, Macmillan Distribution Ltd
Houndmills, Basingstoke, Hampshire RG21 6XS, England

THE POLITICAL HISTORY OF EIGHTEENTH-CENTURY SCOTLAND

John Stuart Shaw

First published in Great Britain 1999 by
MACMILLAN PRESS LTD
Houndmills, Basingstoke, Hampshire RG21 6XS and London
Companies and representatives throughout the world

A catalogue record for this book is available from the British Library.

ISBN 0–333–59585–8 hardcover
ISBN 0–333–59586–6 paperback

 First published in the United States of America 1999 by
ST. MARTIN'S PRESS, INC.,
Scholarly and Reference Division,
175 Fifth Avenue, New York, N.Y. 10010

ISBN 0–312–22430–3

Library of Congress Cataloging-in-Publication Data
Shaw, John Stuart.
The political history of eighteenth-century Scotland / John Stuart
Shaw.
p. cm. — (British history in perspective)
Includes bibliographical references and index.
ISBN 0–312–22430–3 (cloth)
1. Scotland—Politics and government—18th century. I. Title.
II. Series.
DA809.S53   1999
941.1—dc21   99–21982
                                                      CIP

This book is printed on paper suitable for recycling and made from fully managed and
sustained forest sources.

10   9   8   7   6   5   4   3   2   1
08   07   06   05   04   03   02   01   00   99

Printed in Hong Kong

CONTENTS

PREFACE

This book is written from the perspective of the political elite. In this, it reflects the realities of power and influence in the eighteenth century. For those whose preference is the study of emerging popular politics, as far as these are visible to the historian, the book provides an historical background in which such studies can progress.

I would like to thank David Brown, William Bigwood, David Hayton and Laurence Whitley for their great generosity in giving me information and guidance on particular areas of research. I realise that my interpretations on the points in question must inevitably lack their expertise. I must also record the help and encouragement received from the late Peter Vasey. My thanks are due to Roy, Louise and Alec McCluskey, Ishbel Barnes, Jane Brown, Tristram Clarke, Tracy Earl, Karol Gajewski, Rosemary Gibson, Hugh Hagan, Andrew Hanham, Hazel Horn, George MacKenzie, Alex Murdoch and Richard Saville for advice and encouragement so kindly given. I am grateful to the Archives of Coutts & Co. and of the Royal Bank of Scotland and to His Grace the Duke of Roxburghe for allowing me access to their papers. In general, I would like to say how much I appreciate the access that I have received to private papers deposited in archives.

In quoting from original documents I have made a few minor textual changes, particularly to capitalisation and contractions.

Edinburgh, October 1998   J.S.S.

1

THE PRICE OF SCOTLAND?

The main design of this book is to describe the political development of eighteenth-century Scotland after the union. This is viewed from the perspective of those at the top of the political elite. The fiery debate about the 'price of Scotland' gives the reader a flavour of the political world we are entering, or perhaps leaving behind. 'Causes' of the union may be sought in England and in Scotland. The political desirability of bridling a troublesome, vexatious and unreliable neighbour was reason enough on the English side. A particular English aim was to ensure Scottish acceptance of the Hanoverian succession as laid down in the English Act of Settlement of 1701. Among the Scots, for their part, there was some recognition that England called most of the shots and had done so since the union of the crowns. The extreme English reaction to the Darien scheme presented Scots with the harsh reality that an independent Scottish trading empire was an impossible dream. The prospect for the Scots became bleaker still when the Alien Act was passed in 1705. This Act threatened to give Scots the status of aliens and to ban the importation to England of the main articles of Scottish trade if there was not compliance in the matter of the succession.

Meanwhile, in Scotland the country's administration was riven by faction and dispute. It was also showing signs of struggling to survive, having insufficient revenues to meet its needs – and, indeed, there was an underlying balance of payments crisis. On the one hand, there was this sickening prospect. On the other hand, an alluring vista spread out before the Scottish political classes: they had the chance to share in England's trade and prosperity and participate in its political life. In the popular mythology, however, the corruption of the Scottish leadership as *the* 'cause' of the union now tends to exclude all others and is taken to be a self-evident truth. Given the English determination to have the union, bribery was bound to figure. The eighteenth-century world was one in which oiling of the wheels was a natural part of political action. There are also signs of the Scottish leadership taking steps to improve their worldly affairs before the union made it more difficult to do so. And there were just rewards to be received. The honours system that rewarded loyalty and success was an integral part of that aristocratic world. The following account makes other qualifying comments about the price of Scotland, but no final judgement can be made from such an analysis. What follows merely illustrates the background to the allegations that Scotland was bought. It also adds a human dimension.

The method used here is to calculate the financial benefits accruing to those who voted for or against the union in the Scottish parliament. The context of what happened is also important because figures cannot be allowed to speak entirely for themselves. To help give a fuller picture, benefits accruing to people who were not in parliament are mentioned. The figures below are all given in pounds sterling. They have been put together from a selection of records[1] – records in which there are deficiencies and obscurities. The figures are, in short, open to revision. For simplicity's sake the argument is limited to the vote on 'the grand question', that is on the first article of the treaty of union which established that from 1 May 1707 Scotland and England should be united into one kingdom 'by the name of Great Britain'.

George Lockhart of Carnwath, writing about the treaty in his *Memoirs concerning the Affairs of Scotland* (1714), gets to the heart of the matter when he alludes to 'The Equivalent (*alias* Price of Scotland)'. The equivalent is a very complicated subject which, fortunately, has been thoroughly explored by Patrick Riley.[2] The basic equivalent was a sum of £398 085 10s. Under Article 15 of the treaty this was to be paid to Scotland in compensation for Scotland's contribution, itself paid out of customs and excise duties, to England's pre-union national debt. There was also to be a 'rising equivalent'. This was to be paid in compensation for any further increase in the customs and excise duties appropriated to paying off the same debt: the revenues in question would be reviewed after seven years (and thereafter yearly) to see if there had been such an increase. The equivalent, as both of the above measures can be conveniently referred to here, was designed in part to compensate Darien shareholders for losses sustained in the Darien project. The public debts of Scotland were also to be settled. There were other provisions which need not be mentioned in the present context. Lockhart, who had an anti-union Jacobite agenda to promote, said of the equivalent that:

> in Reality it was a swinging Bribe to buy off the Scots Members of Parliament from their duty to their Country, as it accordingly prov'd: For to it we may chiefly ascribe, that so many of them agreed to this Union. The Hopes of recovering what they had expended on the African Company, and obtaining Payment of Debts and Arrears due to them by the Scots Government . . . prevail'd upon many to overcome the general Interest of their Country.[3]

The Darien Stockholders

In disbursing the equivalent, priority was given to Darien payments. The question of priority is important because, first, the claims on the equivalent were greater than the equivalent itself – the latter being based on unrealistic estimates – and, second, the revenues did not achieve the anticipated surpluses. Many creditors therefore ended up with debentures for later redemption rather than with immediate payment. Turning then to the Darien stockholders, the first question is how far the members of parliament – the nobility (including the officers of state), the commissioners for the shires and those for the royal burghs – and their close families were financially involved in the Company of Scotland Trading to Africa and the Indies, the Darien Company. This question can be extended to cover the subscriptions to Darien of the burghs (the royal burghs) represented in parliament. Lack of evidence makes it impractical to extend the analysis further to cover the influence of friends outside parliament on the voting intentions of members of the nobility, or of friends and constituents on the intentions of the commissioners for the shires. Similarly, no account is taken of those who did not attend parliament for the vote approving the first article of the treaty of union. That vote took place on 4 November 1706.

Of the 198 members who voted, 115 were for the union and 83 against. These figures exclude the Earl of Seafield, the lord chancellor, who was not able to attend when the vote was taken, but asked to be included in the list of those who approved. To achieve a correct balance, however, the Duke of Queensberry is added to the figures. He, as high commissioner, the personal representative of the Queen, did not have a vote but led the court, pro-union interest. He was manager of the affair on behalf of the crown. His personal demands on the equivalent were substantial. The voters on Article 1, plus Queensberry, consisted of 67 members of the nobility in parliament (46 for the union, 21 against) including, as officers of state, Adam Cockburn of Ormiston, lord justice clerk, and Sir James Murray of Philiphaugh, lord clerk register. There were 70 commissioners for the shires (37 for, 33 against) and there were 62 commissioners for the burghs (33 for, 29 against). The analysis of their stakes in the Darien Company perhaps raises as many questions as it answers.

The stock of the Darien Company was fixed at £400 000 sterling, to be pledged by subscribers – 'adventurers in the joint stock of the Company'. Subscription books opened on 26 February 1696 and the whole £400 000 was subscribed when these closed on 3 August of that year. Some transfers of stock through the company's books took place between then and the collapse of the enterprise in 1700, and these are allowed for in the following analysis. I calculate that members of parliament who participated in the vote for or against the union and their close families (as far as identified), together with Queensberry, subscribed to £52 700 of the stock, just over a quarter. Subscriptions were to be paid in instalments. The first of these, payable on 1 June 1696, was for a quarter of the subscription. After that there were smaller calls on subscribers, responded to patchily, the last of them on 2 February 1700. The actual money handed over by subscribers came to £153 448. The compensation to be paid to them under the equivalent covered this stock and interest accumulating until 1707, which amounted to £65 646, making a total of £219 094.

In August 1707 a book was opened to record the issue of certificates for sums due to Darien subscribers (and listing other debts due by the company).[4] These certificates were redeemed quickly, the commissioners for the equivalent, who managed claims and payments, testifying in the following February as to their own great forwardness in making payments. Unfortunately, this record of certificates is incomplete. It excludes 19 of the people who voted on the union, and the Duke of Queensberry. He had subscribed £3000, the maximum. The company's cash books assist in arriving at an estimate of the sums due to these members. In Queensberry's case, the stock he had bought in response to calls on subscribers was £1275, which, with interest, would entitle him to a certificate for about £1813. In total, it is calculated that certificates for about £47 270 would have been issued in the names of those involved in the union vote or their families. A disproportionate share of this, £32 614, was in the names those who were 'for' the union. The figures are as follows: 58.29 per cent of the total number of voters and Queensberry were for the union, 41.71 per cent were against. In comparison 69 per cent of the compensation for Darien which was issued in the name of those people went to those for the union, 31 per cent of it to those against.

To the equation can be added the subscriptions pledged to the Darien Company by the burghs whose commissioners took part in the vote. Each of the 66 royal burghs other than Edinburgh sent a commissioner to parliament: Edinburgh sent two. Clearly, the councils who subscribed had a financial interest in the vote and this could influence how their commissioners to parliament voted. This is said with some wariness, because the power of burgh councils to dictate to their commissioners in parliament should not be assumed. Above all, the authority of landed magnates could be a significant outside influence in some places. A graphic suggestion of this is found in the very close relationships of a good 17 of the burgh commissioners to the members of the peerage, some of the latter being major political figures.[5] Among these commissioners were: John Campbell of Burnbank, commissioner for Renfrew, uncle of the Duke of Argyll; William Carmichael of Skirling, commissioner for Lanark, son of the Earl of Hyndford; Sir David Dalrymple of Hailes, Sir George Dalrymple of Dalmahoy and Sir Hew Dalrymple of North Berwick, commissioners for Culross, Stranraer and North Berwick, uncle and brothers respectively of the Earl of Stair (died January 1707); Robert Douglas, commissioner for Kirkwall, who became Earl of Morton in 1715; Sir Andrew Hume of Kimmerghame, commissioner for Kirkcudbright, who was son of the Earl of Marchmont; Roderick Mackenzie of Prestonhall, commissioner for Fortrose, who was brother of the Earl of Cromartie; Patrick Ogilvie of Cairnbulg, commissioner for Cullen, who was son of the Earl of Findlater; and Dugald Stewart of Blairhall, commissioner for Rothesay, who was brother of the Earl of Bute. It would be appropriate to add William Alves, writer in Edinburgh (that is a solicitor), commissioner for Sanquhar, who was Queensberry's man of business, his 'doer', in Edinburgh; and John Clerk, later Sir John Clerk of Penicuik, commissioner for Whithorn, who was Queensberry's pro-tégé. With very few exceptions, this group of people with connections to the peerage voted for the union. The most notable exception was Dugald Stewart. His brother Bute was against the union and did not attend parliament for the vote.

But such outside influences were not all-pervasive and there are signs of councils exercising, or attempting to exercise, independent authority in instructions to their commissioners. On 2 November 1706, the council of Dunbar noted that several burghs were giving instruc-tions to their commissioners about the union. Dunbar recommended that their own commissioner, bailie Robert Kellie, should be written to by the magistrates 'giving him such instructions anent the union as they shall think fitt and convenient'.[6] A most extraordinary exam-ple of an instruction which was not obeyed comes from Brechin. This was one of the smaller royal burghs. Its subscription of £700 to the Darien Company (apart that is from its small share in the subscrip-tion of £3000 by the convention of royal burghs calculated on the basis of the size of the burgh tax rolls) was out of all proportion to the town's significance. This £700 was the fourth largest subscription by a burgh council, that is excluding independent subscriptions from merchant and trades houses and craft incorporations – who also had an interest in burgh affairs.[7] It was exceeded only by £3000 each from Edinburgh and Glasgow and £2000 from Perth. The first £100 of Bre-chin's subscription to Darien came from the common good of the burgh. Then, the minimum subscription being £100, the council of-fered to take in smaller local contributions and submit these as its own. The council in Perth did something similar, 31.5 per cent of its subscription coming from the trade incorporations and 43.5 per cent from leading citizens.[8]

In Brechin's case £50 was contributed by the town's guildry. The remaining £650 came from 41 individuals, 14 of them women. Typi-cal of the latter were: Elizabeth Watt, daughter of the deceased Alexander Watt, merchant in Brechin; Catherine Mill, widow of John Steill, shoemaker there; Elizabeth and Anna Guthrie, daughters of the deceased David Guthrie of Wester Seatone; and Isobel Innes, daughter of the deceased John Innes, physician in Brechin, all of whom contributed £5. A picture is built up of a small, modestly pros-perous community, which faced a tangible loss if the union vote did not open the way to compensation for Darien subscribers. In looking at cause and effect, the conclusion is irresistible that this had a bearing on the act of council of 23 October 1706 which ordered a letter to the burgh's commissioner, Francis Mollison, to be signed by all the members of the council, ordaining that he vote for the union.[9] The wretched Mollison not only voted against the union, he also stuck to his guns after the no vote failed, being in the rump who voted against Article 15, the article which provided for the equivalent.

The councils whose commissioners voted for and against the union (five did not vote) had paid-up Darien stock and interest – from their own subscriptions or their share in the convention of royal burghs' subscription – of £8528. £2030 of this represented votes for and £6498 represented votes against. One of Edinburgh's commissioners, Sir Patrick Johnston, voted for; the other, Robert Inglis, voted against; so the money due to Edinburgh, £2516, is divided here between the burgh yeses and the noes. The figure for the latter is boosted by Glasgow's £2115 and Perth's £1266. Even without this, the overall weight of money in the no camp is striking. Does this suggest altruism on the noes' part, while those who voted yes succumbed to bribery? What is demonstrated rather is the crudity of the bald assumption defining the voting pattern merely in terms of bribery. A good part of the burgh yes vote can be linked to the domination of the landed political elite in some places. Whereas the strong no vote can be attributed in part not to altruism, but to the certainty that Article 22, which said that Scotland would have 45 representatives in the House of Commons, meant that the individual burghs (except Edinburgh, as it happened) would lose their independent representation, an important factor for Glasgow and Perth for example. In general, the voting pattern among the burghs suggests a rather introspected no vote in comparison with wider influences at work in the yes vote. In the case of the two Edinburgh representatives, this was characterised by the no vote of Robert Inglis, the Edinburgh goldsmith representing the trades of the burgh, perhaps an inward-looking group, and the yes vote of the grand former commissioner for the union, Sir Patrick Johnston, representing the merchant elite.

Turning again to the wider picture, there is an element in it which, if taken at face value, might have something to say about the motives of voters on the union. This is the circumstance that some had assigned their Darien stock to other parties. There were assignations of £8345 from the voters, £2189 of this being from those who voted for the union and a disproportionate £6156 being from those who voted against. There were also assignations of £1390 *to* those who voted for and £93 worth to those who voted against. The assignations in question took place sometime between the closure of the company's last call on subscribers in February 1700 and the issuing of certificates for compensation under the equivalent in August 1707. The book dealing with certificates gives the names of assignees and others who received these in place of the original subscribers. What it does not give are the dates on which assignations took place. If an assignation was made before the articles of union were drawn up, or shortly before the voting on the union, particularly on Articles 1 and 15 (the article dealing with the equivalent), these circumstance would be significant. For example, among those who had assigned their stock were leaders of the anti-union lobby, the Duke of Hamilton and Andrew Fletcher of Saltoun. How interesting it would be if they had made assignations before the voting, taking a small return on their investments rather than holding out for more and being seen to profit by the union even when voting against it. The same could be said about 13 others who voted against the union and are known to have assigned their stock (in this respect it may be noted that only eight of the larger group who voted for the union made assignations).

These attractive speculations seem fanciful. There is evidence that it was really only financially worthwhile to make assignations after parliament had voted on Article 15. One cannot be certain, but signs of voters being politically manipulative when making assignations cannot be discerned. Few of the papers of Fletcher survive and they do not give any clues about his assignation. Hamilton's are more promising. In June 1707, when he was in deep financial distress, he was badly advised by his Edinburgh agent that the Bank of England was 'willing to advance the equivalent, and that payment may be made in bank notes'. The implication is that Hamilton still had his Darien stock at that time. He later told his mother, the Duchess Anne, that 'I can take God to witness when a sold my African monie I had not wherwithall to go to the market for dinner to my familly.'[10] A certificate for his stock and interest, value £1208, was issued to John Gordon, writer in Edinburgh, who had right to it 'by progress'.

In looking for further evidence, the most promising sources are the records of minute-keeping bodies. Three such bodies are Brechin burgh council and the incorporations of hammermen and coopers of Glasgow, each one of which assigned away its subscription. The last two of these were not of course involved in the vote, but they still provide useful evidence. On 13 December 1706, after the treaty of

union had been ratified by parliament, the council in Brechin recorded their understanding that subscribers to Darien were to be
recompensed for the payment of a quarter's subscription made to the
company, 'conforme to the articles of union betwixt Scotland and
England . . . upon the first day of May nixt to come'. Therefore they
authorised the provost, Alexander Young, to go to Edinburgh and
negotiate to assign their subscription to the best advantage.[11] An assignation was made to John Gordon for an unspecified sum. Similarly,
on 8 March 1707 a meeting of the hammermen 'surmised' that 'a
transaction may be made' to recover some part of their investment in
Darien. They nominated representatives to deal with anyone who
would 'transact theranent' with them for £42 'or more if they can get
it'. In fact, they received £45.[12] If they had been patient, they would
have redeemed a certificate for £60 8s. in September. Instead, the certificate was delivered to their assignee, John Gordon. In accepting such
a modest sum from him, they had not allowed for their full entitle-
ment to interest.

The coopers' minute book does not mention their transaction, but
their accounts for 1706–September 1708 suggest similar mismanagement on their part. An undated entry records their acceptance of £20
15s. 2d. from Peter Murdoch:[13] the ultimate assignee was John Gordon, who got a certificate for £53 11s. 2d. Unlike the Hamilton example,
these three cases point towards unnecessary haste – following from ignorance as to the actual terms of the equivalent and from relief in getting
something back on Darien investments which had seemed worthless
for years. In retrospect, such a bird-in-the-hand view of things was not
entirely unwise. The funds made immediately available under the
equivalent turned out to be insufficient to meet all demands and,
ultimately, debentures had to be issued to those who had not been
paid. However, public and political pressures were such that the Darien payments were sure to get priority. The dealings involving John
Gordon give a hint of the precipitate assignation of stock after the
equivalent had been approved by parliament, but not always of actual
financial desperation. Gordon, an obscure figure, who is not the John
Gordon associated with the Bank of Scotland at that time, is identifia-
ble as the son-in-law of Robert Kyle, writer to the Signet. Gordon was
the biggest recipient of Darien assignations. In total, 137 certificates
are recorded as delivered to him, with a value of £19 828. Six of these,
worth £3555, were from members of parliament who took part in the
vote (or their families). Among these people were: the Duke of Hamilton,

Andrew Fletcher (£604); the Viscount of Kilsyth (£604); and the Duke of Atholl (£302). Gordon also had a right to Sir John Houston of that ilk's £604, which was arrested, indicating financial embarrassment in this instance.

A whiff of a lack of financial probity among some commissioners is evoked by the fleeting appearance of one Captain Francis Charteris of Her Majesty's Horse Guards among the assignees. Twenty of the Darien certificates, worth about £2000, were delivered to him. Three of these, worth £460, were from people who took part in the vote. In view of Charteris's background, this is enough to raise questions. Known to posterity as Colonel Charteris, he was a cardsharp, moneylender, usurer and, to be fair, extortioner. Such was his enterprise in these fields that he acquired a vast fortune. At his death in 1732, he is said to have had estates valued at about £7000 a year and £100 000 in stocks. He was not, incidentally, without friends, leaving bequests to the following, who also figure in this book: Duncan Forbes of Culloden (£1000 and Stoneyhill House, Musselburgh, rent free for life); Lord Milton (£1000), the second Duke of Argyll (a pair of pistols); and Sir Robert Walpole (Charteris's valuable stable of horses). Less enamoured of him was the Duke of Queensberry. When the latter was in Edinburgh in 1706 on union business, Charteris attended the Duchess's card parties. It is said that he ended by fleecing her of £3000 sterling in one sitting by looking at her cards in a mirror. As a moneylender, he was notorious for charging exorbitant interest, sometimes on mortgages, sometimes on advances to those who had lost to him at cards or dice.[14]

In coming to general conclusions about Darien subscriptions and the union vote, credit may be given to those shareholders who voted against the union, endangering their hopes of redeeming their stock in doing so. But, without going into the complexity of individual motives, it should be remembered that the vote was for a full 'incorporating' union. In the minds of some in Scotland, a vote against would not preclude the negotiation of a looser federal union. In these circumstances, compensation to Darien subscribers would remain on the cards. Perhaps more important are, on the one hand, the relative financial insecurity of those who voted no, as discovered in the assignations, and, on the other hand, the larger stake in Darien of those who voted yes. From this and from what is found in the civil list, it can be gathered that the yes vote was generally more representative of those who were successful within the existing political order – with all the financial rewards that entailed – and who would veer naturally towards the court's pro-union interest without any just imputation of corruption. There is also a contradiction in the crude assumption that the much greater proportion of Darien stock held by those who voted yes than by those who voted no is a graphic demonstration of people selling-out their nation. Stock holdings must have influenced some. It would be surprising if they did not. But the relative proportions also suggest that the greater share of patriotism, when weighed in the balance, resided in those who voted yes. They were, after all, the ones who had shown their patriotism. It was they who had invested in Darien, the great national enterprise, whereas so many of those who voted no had held on to their purses.

The Public Debts

The next question is to assess how far members of parliament were corruptly influenced by the prospect of the public debts of Scotland being paid by means of the equivalent. Scotland did not have a national debt as such. What is referred to here are payments due as far back as William and Mary's accession in 1689 on the civil list; and payments on what the commissioners for the equivalent called 'the Second General Account', mainly covering sums owing to the military. To temper sweeping judgements about corruption and unpatriotic motives, it is as well to remember that the lists in question included small pensioners who could have no say or influence on decisions about the union. For example, the equivalent commissioners issued certificates for relatively small sums to people on the civil list, such as £15, £20 or £30 to those on Her Majesty's charity roll, described as the 'Charity &c Second Class Civil List', many of them widows. About 180 of the recipients were female and 30 of them male.

There were also big military arrears. These hardly affected the members of parliament who voted on the union, often involving uninfluential people who were justly entitled to payment without being pilloried as traitors to their country. There were 112 certificates issued on the second general account, which I calculate at just under £11 000, more than three-quarters of which was for military purposes. These certificates, sometimes issued to heirs or assignees, covered arrears of pay, such as £10 to John Murray, gunner at Fort William, and £48 17s. 10d. to the late Lord Forbes, captain of a troop of horse; miscellaneous payments, including £100 to James Hepburn for the passage of troops over the River Spey and £85 17s. 8½d. to the Invalides; and payments for the clothing and subsistence of troops. The two biggest military certificates were issued to someone who was not in parliament, the son of Sir William Douglas. One was for £1538 for Sir William's arrears of pay as a brigadier general. The other was for £1391 to cover clothing money for his regiment. The regiment was disbanded after the treaty of Ryswick in 1697, when large sums were owing to Sir William for subsistence and arrears. Then, following the renewal of hostilities with France in 1701, his estate in France was confiscated. In 1703 he petitioned parliament 'that something may be done to keep him and his family from starving'.

Turning to the great and good of Scotland, the key elements of the equivalent affecting them, apart from the Darien payments, were on an altogether different scale. First, there was £30 500 in fees due to the Scottish commissioners (and their officials) who took part in the abortive union negotiation of 1702–3 and the successful negotiation of 1706. £26 600 of this £30 500 is ascribed to people who took part in the vote on the first article of union in 1706 and to Queensberry (£1500); £25 100 going to those who were for the union, £1500 to those who were against. Payment to them was made by the end of 1707.[15] Next, there was £24 736 owing to high commissioners to parliament for their equipage money and daily allowances (covering their salaries and expenses). The equivalent commissioners are said to have handed this over sometime before February 1709. £22 986 of it went to Queensberry, who was high commissioner in 1700, 1702 and 1703, and the remaining £1750 to the Marquis of Tweeddale, who was high commissioner in 1704 and voted for the union in 1706. Then there were certificates for £80 418, issued from February 1709, to those who were on what the equivalent commissioners called the first and third classes of the civil list, covering the fees, salaries and pensions of ministers and officials and some other public debts. Most 'pensions' were salaries rather than annuities for the retired. It is calculated that £39 161 of this sum was owing to the members of parliament who voted on the union and to Queensberry (£2270 for pensions as lord privy seal and as a lord of the treasury, Scotland, 1706–7) or to their immediate families; £30 878 of it going to those for the union, £8283 to those against.

Out of a total of £135 654 covering this last group of equivalent payments and certificates, I calculate therefore that the proceeds to those who took part in the union vote and to Queensberry were

£90 497; of which £80 714 went to those for and £9783 to those against. These sums were all the more disproportionate when compared with the numbers who voted for and against. There is more to be discovered from the figures. First, there was relatively little put at risk by the leadership of the opposition to the union. The Duke of Hamilton and Andrew Fletcher of Saltoun had nothing due to them. The Duke of Atholl, not initially the most consistent opponent of the union, had £1500 to receive as lord privy seal, 1703–4. The Marquis of Annandale, secretary of state in 1705, had £500 to come to him as a union commissioner in 1702. Lockhart himself had £500 to come to him as a union commissioner in 1706. Other significant sums to those who voted against the union were £1400 to the Earl of Buchan; £1200 to John Forbes of Culloden, commissioner to parliament from the county of Nairn (a sum originally due to his late father); and £1300 due to the father of John Sinclair younger of Stevenson, one of the commissioners for Lanarkshire.

Excluding Darien payments, some important people in favour of the union actually had no claim on the equivalent at all. Among them were the Marquis of Montrose and the Earl of Roxburghe.

In drawing conclusions from the above features of the equivalent as a provision to pay off arrears in Scotland, it would be wise to keep in mind that it was negotiated as compensation to Scotland for taking on a share of England's national debt. The simple fact that there were – that there had to be – proper fiscal arrangements in the treaty undermines the more crude definitions of the equivalent as a wicked bribe. The Scots who negotiated the union would have been mad and incompetent if they had not made provision in the treaty for their own country's public debts. It is poignant that these debts would, if not catered for, have left relatively humble individuals and their families distressed. Of course the bulk of this part of the equivalent went to more powerful people and that had to be the case, given that a large share of the public debts of Scotland was made up of outstanding fees and pensions to past and present members of the administration and officials. It may be deplored by those of a passionate egalitarian disposition that the landed classes, including members of the ruling elite, were the principal beneficiaries, but such an outcome was obviously unavoidable given the nature of society at the time.

There is something more subtle to be drawn from the figures, something which has as much to do with the economic reasons for union as with questions of bribery and corruption. An uneasy sense begins to arise that the union was negotiated when all was not well with Scottish public revenues and hence with the national economy. Arrears of fees and pensions are not a surprise in themselves and were not unknown after the union, especially for those out of political favour, but in some cases among those who voted the time-scale suggests a problem. For example, sums owing to the lord justice clerk, Adam Cockburn of Ormiston, included £554 for his pay as treasurer depute in 1702–3; the Earl of Buchan had pension arrears of £1400 for 1696–1701 and 1706–7; there were pensions totalling £2300 due to the Earl of Forfar and his son Lord Wandell for 1699–1706; the Earl of Glencairn awaited a pension of £650 for 1697–1701; £2000 was sought by the Earl of Kintore, knight marischal, including a payment for 1689; Alexander Abercrombie of Glasshaugh, a commissioner to parliament for Banffshire, awaited £450 for 1696–1700 as Lady Jean Hay's assignee. It was common for royal warrants for specific payments to be sent to the Scottish treasury year after year, and for payment not to be made. The conclusion must be that revenues were not there to cover them. There are signs in the years before the union therefore of payments being prioritised and of essential ones being allocated to more secure parts of the revenue. These are the reasons why so much of the civil list debt covered by the equivalent was owing to people who were outwith the top notches of the power structure and were yesterday's men.

Two suspicious circumstances follow from this. One is that those who had to be rewarded for their services in furthering the union were often taken care of by more immediate and sure means than the equivalent, at least whenever practical; not always, it must be said, before the union vote took place. The other is that, in contrast, some weaker people were placed in a dependent position at the time of the union vote, having to rely on the equivalent with all the uncertainties and delays that entailed. This, it may be imagined, was because of their relatively low places in the pecking order rather than through cynical manipulation. There are reasonable grounds for justifying the disparity between the two groups, the powerful tending by nature to look after their own interests first, without having to have any great political motive to do so. Equally, however, despite all my caveats, a dark picture emerges in the benefits received outside the equivalent.

Other Awards

A telling example of what was happening outwith the equivalent is that of Daniel Campbell of Ardentenny, later of Shawfield. He was commissioner for the burgh of Inveraray, Argyll's seat. In 1696 he received an order from the Scottish treasury for £700 'in consideration of several great losses sustained by him and his partners in their trade' during hostilities with France. He had still not received payment at the start of August 1706, three months before the union vote. On 12 August a royal warrant was issued for him to be paid out of the tack duty of the Scottish customs and excise, of which he was one of the tacksmen. Another striking coincidence, one of quite a number of these, was the renewal of a royal charter of the earldom of Orkney to the Earl of Morton in early 1707. In 1669 following a decree of the court of session, parliament had abrogated the original disposition and a later confirmation of the islands of Orkney and Shetland to the Earls of Morton. The earldom was considered in 1669 'so great a jewel of the Crown', too valuable a royal gift for a subject to receive. *The Scots Peerage* observes that: 'This iniquitous Act, one of the most disgraceful ever passed by the Scots Parliament, not only caused great loss, if not absolute ruin to the Morton family, but involved other creditors who had lent the Earl money on the security of lands, of which he had a valid title from the Crown.'[16] More striking still are a number of peerages granted to those who promoted the union. Argyll was created Earl of Greenwich in the English peerage after his time as high commissioner. This guaranteed him a seat in the House of Lords after the union, when, under Article 22, only 16 members of the Scots peerage were to be elected to sit there. His brother, Lord Archibald Campbell, was made Earl of Ilay (modern spelling Islay) in the Scots peerage shortly before the union vote. This qualified him to be one of 'the 16' and to be a member of the union parliament (in which he acted as treasurer). Lord Henry Scott, younger son of Anne, Duchess of Buccleuch and the Duke of Monmouth, was made Earl of Deloraine and voted yes in the union parliament, as well as being an active lord commissioner of the Scottish treasury at that time. Montrose and Roxburghe were rewarded with dukedoms in the Scots peerage in April 1707, just a week before the union. And in May 1708 Queensberry was created Duke of Dover in the post-union British peerage.

It is convenient to add here a pension of £3000 a year granted to Queensberry out of post-office revenues in May 1707, 'in consideration of good, faithful and acceptable services and as a mark of royal favour'. Seafield was granted a pension of £3000 in September 1708 and the Earl of Mar also received a pension of £3000 in that year, but these are too late to have significance in terms of the union vote. Also of importance, but easy to overlook in assessing things, there are in the state papers for months before the union a spate of warrants for grants of royal charters under the Great Seal and gifts out of crown rents and property. These grants were commonly made to those who voted for the union, but not only to them. Morton's is the most important example of charters granted. An example at the opposite end of the scale was a charter to the Earl of Rosebery of the islet of Inchgarvie in the Forth estuary. Inchgarvie did not produce any rents for the crown, but was a useful acquisition for Rosebery who had lands on either side of the Forth. It was granted 'for the many good and faithful services done and performed by the said Earl and his predecessors' to the Queen and her predecessors. Among the other gifts, the most common were of feu duties. Taking April 1707 for example, Roxburghe got a gift for life of the feu, blench and other duties of the lordship of Kelso from Whitsunday 1704 and worth about £94 a year; the Earl of Haddington got a gift of the same duties for the lordship of Melrose, Coldstream and Binning for the same period, worth £118 a year; and William Morison of Prestongrange, commissioner for Peeblesshire, got a gift of the duties on his lands for 19 years from Martinmas 1706, amounting to £29 a year and a discharge for all sums resting.

Another reward went through less formal channels. This was the secret payment of £20 000 to Queensberry shortly before he left London for the union vote. In 1711 there was an accounts commissioner's investigation into the affair.[17] Lockhart was later to seize on the payment as a prime example of the corruption that attended the union. The £20 000 was given to Queensberry for distribution, to ease the passage of the union. The first damning aspect of this affair is its secrecy: the transaction was not entered in the official accounts. The second is that Queensberry kept £12 325 of this money for equipage and daily allowance, yet his arrears – which came to almost twice that amount – remained without any deduction on the civil list and were presumably paid. Queensberry is said to have offered back the overpayment later.[18] A lesser aspect is that a number of the people who received much smaller payments out of the £20 000, most of them voters for the union, did not have any arrears in the civil list. In other words, these seemed to be straight cash payments to secure their votes. A few of them voted no. A transaction that is hardly less murky is identified by William Ferguson. This involved the group known as the new party or squadrone. Part of their price for supporting the court's measures was that they would be given the oversight of disbursing the part of the equivalent dedicated to compensating the Darien shareholders. The squadrone were tricked. Ferguson thinks it unlikely that the court ever intended to honour this pledge, such were the powers of patronage it conferred. Once the treaty of union had been converted into an act of parliament, the court reneged. It insisted that there should be a commission for the equivalent to manage claims and payments. The commission was to be answerable to the British parliament.[19] Resentment about this will have carried over into the post-union period.

2

THE POLITICS OF GREAT BRITAIN

Background

The union was finally achieved through the will in England of Lord
Treasurer Godolphin and his allies the Whig Junto lords and, in Scotland, through the brief alliance of Queensberry, the Duke of Argyll
and the squadrone. Such co-operation was all the more significant
because in those times, politics were enlivened by faction, hatred, jealousy and self-interest. It was the same in both kingdoms without regard
to party affiliations. George Lockhart, who had been a member of
the Scottish Privy Council, referred to Scotland before the union as a
country riven by 'court divisions, pairties and animosities among no-
bles'. No doubt England's grandeur and gravitas, in comparison with
Scotland's ramshackle instability on the margins of Europe, gave the
antics of the Scottish pre-union elite a wild, unruly air; but the English were almost their match: 'the English itch of contentione, the
worst plague that poor Scotland was ever yet overspread with' was an
opinion from north of the border in 1708.[1] So matters continued in
disputatious vein in one form or another after the union. This was
sometimes against the backdrop in England of divisions at court, a
succession of long-term quarrels between the kings and their eldest
sons, the Princes of Wales. For special reasons, however, the impact
on Scottish affairs was disproportionately severe; whereas in England,
the appearance was worse than the reality.

The obtrusiveness of personal clashes and faction upon the politics of the century in Great Britain followed, in part, from the absence of formal party organisation. It followed also from frustrated ambitions in the battle to control or receive offices and the other forms of government patronage upon which the prosperity of individuals commonly depended: 'Those out/ May pout/ Those in/ Will grin', wrote Henry Carey in 1727 in his *Lilliputian Ode on their Majesties' Accession*. The split between ins and outs was not always quite as clear as this. In the ebb and flow of politics, there were many that were not quite in favour but had to be given some recognition. Another feature of the spoils system was that it encouraged discontented elements to coalesce round the heir to the throne, the Prince of Wales, against the court (the King's ministry), almost institutionalising opposition. But it should not be inferred from this that, as tends to be assumed, there was an unusual congenital predisposition in the Hanoverian kings and their heirs to fall out with each other. As Romney Sedgwick explains, the peculiarity lay with the political system, not with the royal family. Those out of power could gamble on turning to the prince in hope of rewards when he succeeded to the throne. In Sir Robert Walpole's words: 'Everybody comes to a court to get, and if they find there is nothing to be got in present, it is natural to look out for reversions' (a reversion in legal terms being the right to possess or succeed to property on the death of the present possessor). The older the King got, the stronger the incentive was for opposition to focus on the Prince. For the Prince, heading opposition was, says Sedgwick, 'a safe, effective and agreeable means' of wringing concessions from his father and addressing grievances.[2]

The obtrusiveness of animosity and faction followed also from the complacency of the ruling landed order, complacency which gave it the security to indulge its squabbles. This, at least, showed the system to be maturing sufficiently to allow for division and the settling of scores without the sort of drastic repercussions that would have followed in the previous century. Of course vendettas continued throughout the century – to the bitter end of it, in fact, in the unsuccessful impeachment in 1806 of Henry Dundas, Viscount Melville, for malversion in the use of funds when he was treasurer of the navy. The disappearance of the polarity between Whigs and Tories early in the reign of George III, who wanted to see an end to party divisions, did not improve matters, as it was replaced by increased political faction. On the other hand, colonial and economic expansion improved opportunities outside the political field, so reducing the importance of political preferment; while the radical threat to the status quo in the 1790s served to concentrate minds and allowed personal grievances to have greater subservience to genuine matters of policy.

From the above, it should not be assumed that ideological issues and genuine party differences were unimportant earlier in the century. It is true that the big party divide between conservatism and liberalism emerged fully only in the nineteenth century. Signs of this were developing tentatively in the late eighteenth century, in the competition between those with reformist credentials – the Foxite Whigs – and the conservative forces of the Pitt government and its supporters. Indeed, in the later part of the century, it is only useful to use the term Whig in the reformist context, while the term Tory, used to describe conservative or reactionary individuals, is best avoided then as it serves only to confuse. It is also true, turning again to the early days, that the Whigs and Tories in England had set aside, at least temporarily, the greatest of their traditional differences at 'the glorious revolution'. The Tories, 'a court party which had deserted its king' as Brian Hill describes them,[3] joined with the Whigs, upholders of the doctrine of limited constitutional monarchy, in rejecting King James. The Tory Lord Bolingbroke later reminded readers of his *Dissertation on Parties* that the Tories had participated in the revolution. However, even the apparent acceptance in Tory circles in 1714 of George I's accession did not altogether dissipate suspicions at court and among the Whigs that Tories remained Jacobites at heart. Lord Wharton of the Junto, for one – the Whig party manager at the time of the union (and a man related to the Jacobite George Lockhart[4]) – had been unshakeable in his convictions that they were Jacobite. Robert Walpole, George I and George II were no less convinced: even the dismal Tory response in England to the Jacobite calls to arms in 1715 and 1745 could not change the minds of these gentlemen in that regard, although George I was by nature a conciliator.

Modern research suggests that the Whigs and the two Georges were right, that Jacobite sympathies among the Tories were widespread. There were other party differences in England. One of the most important of these was the Whig sympathy for the protestant dissenters – again represented at its most vigorous by Wharton, whose father, a Puritan, had been a close friend of Cromwell's – contrasting with the Tory championship of the Church of England. This division began to fade under Sir Robert Walpole. Another difference was that the Whigs, dominated though they were by aristocrats, were linked through their support for religious dissent to the mercantile and financial community in the City of London; whereas the Tories, who were in a parliamentary minority from 1715, were associated with the squirearchy of the shires. G. M. Trevelyan famously describes the noisy battle between the Tory landed interest and the Whig monied interest as being largely 'a matter of party cries and shibboleths'; yet the Whig connection with the City undoubtedly helped tap a source for public finance through long-term loans. These loans helped, for example, to finance William III and II soon after his accession to the throne, when England and Holland entered the War of the League of Augsburg against France. The loans for warfare had, of course, to be paid for through taxation.

War and foreign policy were indeed consuming political concerns for much of the century. Such concerns were not only those of the insular Tory gentry. The latter were fuelled with resentment by the effect war was having on the land tax, especially war seen to be in pursuit of the Continental objectives of the first two Georges as electors of Hanover (or, indeed, those previously of William of Orange in his mission to contain the power of France). The taxation and national debt which war engendered bore critically on the conduct of government. They impinged no less on Pitt the Younger at the time of the revolutionary wars – when Britain's military and diplomatic policy in Europe and the colonies was dominated by a 'counting-house spirit'[5] – than they did on Walpole, who aimed to keep taxes low through preserving the peace. Other aspects of foreign policy were the promotion of Great Britain's trading interests and the search for 'the just balance' or 'the equilibrium of Europe'.

At home there was also the Whig concept of the ancient constitutional ideal. This was represented by the balance between the crown, lords and commons, combined with notions about the liberties enjoyed by Saxon freemen.[6] The philosophy was upheld in its most pristine form by the purest of the Whigs. Even while the Whig hegemony lasted during the reigns of the first two Georges, there was no possibility of conforming to such a concept, however, and it was not observed by the Whig leadership. Thus an aim of the Junto lords was the promotion of their faction's power. The overweening exercise of ministerial or executive power, such as Robert Walpole was accused of, also undermined the principle. And the royal dream, a feature of the century, of having pliant ministries of 'king's friends', contradicted it.

Such aberrations were reflected in the division of the Whigs into supporters of 'court' and 'country'. The court and country divide also crossed party lines, with the Tories from the accession of George I being on the country side. In broad terms, those in power at any given time and their adherents were 'court'; those in opposition favoured the 'country' platform. This platform was a form of coalition, but not a stable one. The coalition masked party differences and the membership fluctuated depending on people's political fortunes. The patriotic credentials of the country label were convenient in a century in which outright opposition to ministers appointed by the King smacked of a lack of patriotism.[7] In this respect, a most persuasive, yet facile, political idea was promoted in the 1730s by Bolingbroke in his attack on his hated enemy, Walpole. Bolingbroke argued that more had to be done to complete the 'glorious design' of the revolution. This was to work for a commonwealth devoid of party and faction. The virtuous country would be presided over by a patriot king commanding the universal affection of his subjects. The notion, which long outlived the cause that inspired it, was enthusiastically championed by the country opposition to Walpole, both Whig and Tory, and succeeded in achieving the immediate aim of Bolingbroke and the leader of the opposition, William Pulteney, of encouraging discontent against the ministry.

So concerns for the public interest and for the constitution could be a cloak for less honourable intentions or self-deception, or could show true idealism. This is an example of the confusion that we are faced with in deciding between petty motives and altruism. Amidst the factions and feuds, the underlying issues and concepts in English politics should not be forgotten. Equally, it should be remembered that self-seeking opposition could and did assume the mask of virtue, and those in power could use the appeal of patriotism and civic virtue to achieve political ends. Regarding 'the patriots' in opposition in the 1730s, Sir John Clerk of Penicuik had no doubt: 'They pretended to be great Patriots, and to stand up chiefly in defence of the rights and privileges of the subjects; in a word, the publick good and the liberty of the subjects were still in their mouths, but in their Hearts they were known to have Court preferments and places in the chiefest degree of veneration.'[8]

The other notion was one promulgated and popularised by Bolingbroke during the opposition of the 1730s, and taken on board by Tom Paine later in the century. This was that party divisions were corrupt or, more accurately, one step worse than corruption. 'To corrupt and to divide are trite and wicked expedients', wrote Bolingbroke. Corruption was the less challenging of the two: 'Every busy, ambitious child of fortune, who hath himself a corrupt heart, and becomes master of a large purse, hath all that is necessary to employ the expedient of CORRUPTION with success.' But in order to divide, said Bolingbroke, 'there is need of that left-handed wisdom, called cunning, and those habits of business, called experience.' This was because: 'to divide or to maintain and renew the division of parties in a state, a system of seduction and fraud is necessary to be carried on. The divided are so far from being accessory to the guilt that they would not be divided, if, they were not first deceived.'[9] His popular teaching on party spirit would have eliminated modern party democracies.

Scotland

The Scots who joined the political fray in London had their own factional backgrounds with which to contend. Riley expresses the jaundiced view, a not uncommon one, that the Scottish magnates and their followers were devoid of responsibility for anything except their own prospects. He also contends that the Scots were slowly accommodating themselves to the English two-party structure of Queen Anne's reign and, through time, would have been 'absorbed' into the two-party system in England – had not the rising of 1715 (the '15) ended the prospects of those leaning towards the Tory side in Scotland once and for all. Taken together, Riley's claims suggest that the Scots were without Whig and Tory allegiances when the union took effect and that their leaders were too unprincipled to be troubled by such niceties. As for popular opinion, William Ferguson argues that the masses were politicised before the union, but quickly lost touch with parliamentary politics after it and removal of the legislature to London.[10] David Hayton, however, reassesses the above opinions on the party issue and looks at the period 1708–15 to show the early emergence of Tory and Whig party alignments in Scotland. In doing so, he selects evidence to demonstrate the vitality of certain types of issue. It is impossible to do any sort of justice to his argument in a few words. The feature to be stressed, however, is the Tory and Whig party alignment that quickly appeared, the Tories being drawn from the Episcopalian side and the Whigs from the Presbyterian one. In constituencies where such party issues were to the fore at elections, a 'popular interest' sometimes appeared of lesser lairds whose party loyalties were such that they were able to overcome the firmly established electoral influence of local magnates.

When Hayton turns to the scene in London among the great politicians, he refers to the alliances that were formed between Scottish and English interests. From the point of view of this book, the most interesting feature he discerns is the religious 'tinge' of the squadrone and the track-record of that group of noblemen in following 'principles of civil liberty and parliamentary independence'. In other words, the squadrone displayed Whiggish features and these developed when the alliance the squadrone formed with the Whig Junto, originally a tactical one, continued.[11] One of the squadrone leaders, Montrose, was of a different background, but his father died in his infancy and he was raised to follow sound protestant principles. The squadrone, incidentally, got their nickname 'squadrone volante' before the union (when they were also called the new party) because of the way in which they kept out of permanent alliance with other parties. Their association with the Junto began in 1707 after the union and they quickly merged into the Whig mainstream. They were the enemies of the Duke of Argyll and his friends.

As for Argyll and his brother, the Earl of Ilay, the other long-term Scottish participants in the political struggle in the decades after the union, Hayton joins Riley and Ferguson in wasting no time on their party principles. Argyll is the Scottish magnate *par excellence* (matched only by Queensberry and Hamilton, the two Dukes who died a few years after the union). I believe, however, that there is no difficulty in identifying him as a Whig. George Lockhart, a friend from childhood of Argyll and Ilay, told the Pretender in 1718 that the brothers had 'hitherto bended all their thoughts towards that brand of trade [politics] in which they were educated [Whiggism]'.[12] Argyll (Lord Lorne) was at a young age given command of a regiment (raised by his father) in Flanders by King William. Lorne's travelling tutor was an arch-Whig, Alexander Cunningham. Robert Harley's informant in Amsterdam, John Drummond, of the trading firm Van der Heiden and Drummond, advised Harley in 1710, with reference to the Electress Sophia and the Argyll family, that 'they adore that family at Hanover, for the Duke of Argyll has done more honour to the old Lady's recommendations than any other great man.'[13] It is equally true that Lord Godolphin said in the same year that Argyll was 'one of the greatest favourites' next to the Duke of Somerset at the court of Queen Anne.[14] That, however, does not destroy Argyll's excellent Whig credentials. He fitted the bill as a Whig, although he was too subject to court and personal influences and altogether too grand to be described as a good example of that breed. It has to be conceded that he was ruled by a fearsome temperament. It was this more than his political philosophy that was the spring of his actions and contributed much to the course of Scottish politics until his death in 1743.

More will be said about Ilay's principles or lack of them in Chapter 6. However, his basically Whig outlook is taken for granted from the outset, just as Lockhart understood it. It is true that Ilay was fond of aphorisms about politics as a game of chance, a game which he enjoyed playing. He played it to the full as the political manager of Scotland from 1725 to 1742 (on behalf of Walpole) and from 1746 to 1761 (initially on behalf of Henry Pelham). He no less enjoyed playing chess with the chess master Alexander Cunningham (not the same person as the above), who was a regular visitor to his house in London. The two activities, politics and chess, were probably on a par for Ilay. It is also true that he was very determined in building up the Argyll family interest, and he did so relentlessly. Yet he was a man with great intellectual interests; so there is every reason to believe he had underlying political attitudes if not principles. And the least that can be said is that he was committed to the revolution settlement and the house of Hanover.

The most satisfactory overview, therefore, is to consider that Scotland fitted comfortably into the Whig hegemony that began in 1714 upon the accession of George I. A difficulty arises with this in that there is a view that a preponderance of the Scottish politicians, certainly in mid century, could be considered 'king's men' naturally inclined to support the government, the term 'party' being an alien concept to them.[15] This, of course, is a convenient generalisation and one may reflect on the incident of 1755, mentioned below, in which Newcastle, the first lord of the treasury, had to backtrack because of lack of Scottish support. There is justice in the point nevertheless. But the context has to be remembered. By the middle of the century, the Jacobite challenge had gone, the Hanoverian succession was firmly in place and the Presbyterian form of church government was accepted. The challenges had already been met. Meanwhile, the old party divide was also disappearing at Westminster and it shattered after George III's accession.[16] In the later decades Whiggism became associated with a reforming spirit, but that, much as it was rooted in traditional Whiggish values, was not quite the same thing as was being fought for earlier in the century. In other words, there was an absence of real party issues around which Scots could coalesce in the 1750s and 1760s. As for the abiding impression in Scottish history books that Scottish politics suffered from the selfish and sterile influence of the magnates in the decades after the union, principally that of Argyll, one could not disagree with this totally.

The singular personality of the 'princely Argyll' made a great impact, heightening the influence of personal issues in Scottish politics to an exceptional degree. He was charming and eloquent, but also impetuous and racked by pride and jealousy. The impact of this was all the more severe in that he acted at the centre of London politics, as did other prominent Scots. In Westminster and Whitehall there were even more powerful figures – the likes of Lord Sunderland – who could be equally vicious in their enmity. Another factor in Argyll's background and that of his brother was a coolness towards them in the court of George II, brought about by their own behaviour. This confined their political power, restricting them in what they could do to advance the cause of Scotland. The blight was potentially all the more damaging because of the long period in which they held sway there. However, Chapter 3 suggests that factional and personal infighting between their English associates was no less severe; indeed, the Scottish and English rivalries became intertwined. We need therefore to take a closer look to understand the relative trivialisation or sterility of Scottish politics at elite level.

The Duke of Montrose, a leader of the squadrone, remarked in 1719 that: 'Private anemosityes are often the springs of great changes.' In the politics of England private animosities were, as observed, only one factor in the equation, such were the great affairs that prevented them from dominating. In the politics of Scotland, in so far as Scotland had its separate politics, animosities were certainly more obtrusive for many years after the union. They represented the aforesaid trivialisation of Scottish politics. This state of affairs was not simply down to magnate influences. In was brought about, in part, because the Scots were excluded from a significant share in government at ministerial level outside Scottish matters. For much of the century, Scots did not even have formal control of Scottish business. In 1708–9 the main remnants of the old structure of government in Scotland were dismantled. This happened with the abolition first of the Privy

Council and then of the office of Scottish secretary of state. The secretaryship was held jointly at the union by the Earl of Loudoun, who
resigned in May 1708, and the Earl of Mar, who was dismissed in
February 1709. From then, with the important qualification regarding the post of third British secretary mentioned below, there was,
strictly speaking, no post of Scottish secretary until the office was re-
established in 1925.

During the eighteenth century, until 1782 when the posts of home
and foreign secretaries were created, home and foreign affairs in England were the shared responsibility of two secretaries of state, for the
southern and northern departments. The secretary for the north also
tended to look after Scottish affairs (outside treasury business) during the greater part of the century after 1707, until the home secretary
took over in 1782. A major exception was in the regime of the tena-
cious Duke of Newcastle. He managed Scottish business when secretary
for the southern department, 1724 to the beginning of 1742, briefly
again in early 1746, and then as secretary for the northern department until 1754. In the early days, the heads of the ministry, first
Godolphin, then Robert Harley, Earl of Oxford, directly controlled
Scottish business for a time; and in the middle 1750s the Duke of
Newcastle interfered much in Scottish politics when first lord of the
treasury. Only for relatively short spells did Scots at Westminster have
official responsibility for Scottish business. In 1709 the Duke of
Queensberry was appointed to the new position of third secretary of
state of Great Britain, which virtually amounted to the Scottish secretaryship by another name. He held it until his death in 1711, when it
lapsed. It was reintroduced in 1713, when Mar held it until the accession of George I. It was used three more times, when squadrone peers,
the Dukes of Montrose and Roxburghe and the Marquis of Tweeddale held it in 1714–15, 1716–25 and 1742–46 respectively.

There were only three other times when Scots had fully validated
authority over Scotland. The first was under Lord Bute, as secretary
for the northern department, 1761–62, then as first lord of the treasury, 1762–63. He delegated his authority to his brother, James Stuart
Mackenzie, the 'minister for Scotland'. The second was under Lord
Stormont as secretary for the northern department, 1779–82. The
third was under Henry Dundas as home secretary, 1791–94. Dundas
was also the political manager of Scotland on behalf, first, of Lord
Shelburne and, from the end of 1783, on behalf of Pitt the Younger.
Historians often refer to some lesser Scottish offices as being a form of

recognition of the recipients' authority in controlling Scotland. The cases in question include the keepership of the Signet when held by Mar, the keepership of the Privy Seal when held by Lord Ilay and the post of lord advocate whoever held it. In fact, these positions did not carry clear recognition of authority. The first two were sinecures, offices with handsome perquisites. Perhaps only when James Stuart Mackenzie held the Privy Seal – under Bute and, for a time, under Grenville – could that office be recognised unequivocally as a mark of ministerial authority in Scottish affairs; and the lord advocate's post was a relatively minor one without genuine political authority until Henry Dundas began in the 1770s to make a great deal of it. As for the status of Scots in politics outwith Scotland, for decades after the union they were not found at the inner core of government. A memorandum on Mar's appointment as third secretary speaks for itself: 'that though for saving appearances he has the usual form of a Secretary of Great Britain yet the Queen understands that he is to meddle with nothing but the affairs of Scotland, and his Lordship acquiesces therein.' It was further stated that he was not to have anything to do with army commissions in Scotland.[17] Mar, with his Jacobite leanings, was the least accepted of the third secretaries.

There are signs that the others could make a limited contribution to the wider scene. Scots were to be found on the Privy Council. Those who operated in the reigns of the first two Georges were also to be found among the lords justices, a committee of regency which acted during the visits of the monarch to Hanover. However, Jeremy Black observes that during the first half of the century, there were no Scots in the inner cabinet in which government policy was formulated.[18] It may be added that the few prominent homebred Scots in the House of Commons in the half century or so after the union – people such as George Baillie, Gilbert Elliot and James Oswald – were no more successful than any of the great lords before Bute in rising to the top. In general, the most significant feature of the scene was the non-participation of senior Scottish politicians before Bute in foreign affairs, the most important political business. The only glimmer of a responsibility was a political concession by Godolphin to Queensberry in 1710. An arrangement was reached in which the fees of the three secretaries were pooled and Queensberry was given charge of relations with Russia, Poland, Denmark and Sweden.[19]

A number of factors contributed to marginalising Scots and hence to trivialising their politics, at worst, or limiting their flair, at best, for many decades. One aspect was the dominant influence of peers in Scottish politics – particularly the influence of Argyll, Ilay and Bute which ended in 1763 – but in a different sense than that of the destructive magnate behaviour mentioned above. The aspect in question concerns the relative importance of the House of Commons and the House of Lords. Great though the power of the aristocracy was in Britain throughout the century, in terms of parliamentary politics strength lay, ultimately, with the House of Commons, as demonstrated by the careers of Walpole, Henry Pelham and the two Pitts, whose success sprang from mastery of that chamber. The dominant role in the political life of Scotland of great lords after the union tended to suppress the potential of its MPs, thereby frustrating political development.

At first sight, it seems that there was recognition by the Scottish noblemen in London in the 1760s and 70s that they did not have the role they would like to have in the politics of the country, with a significant number of them returning to Scotland from that time to concentrate on the improvement of their estates.[20] From the late 1780s to the 1790s, however, there was actually an appreciable increase in attendances by Scots in the House of Lords;[21] so the peers evidently did not recognise a decline in their importance. I would point to an economic reason in preference to a political one for the exodus of the 1760s–70s, or, indeed, in preference to the role of 'civic virtue' in encouraging interest in improvement. T. M. Devine explains how the commitment of landowners to improvement in that era followed from expectations of 'hugely increased profits' on their investments in a relatively short time. This related to the accelerating commercialisation of agriculture and the 'gearing of outlay to rent increases'. This was a time when paternalism in the Scottish countryside was under great pressure.[22] Even the more refined and cultured improvements to houses, parks and grounds depended, first and foremost, on the availability of hard cash. Leaving this matter aside, the political potential of the Scots was only discovered when their leadership came into the hands of Henry Dundas, an exceptional performer in the House of Commons. Even if Ilay had the same political flair as Dundas, he could never, as a member of the House of Lords, have been as influential. It is true there was a great aristocrat successfully involved in Scottish politics in Dundas's day. That was the Duke of Buccleuch. But he was in Scotland – in partnership with his friend Dundas in building up and maintaining an interest there.

Another fundamental reason for the trivialisation of Scottish politics until quite late in the century was that British or English political considerations dominated the agenda from the elevated realms of foreign affairs to the lowly reaches of factional dispute. It was in any case customary in English ruling circles to treat Scotland as subservient. This followed naturally from the relative strength of the two countries. It was summed up in a comment by Ilay to Oxford in 1713: 'Our affairs even before the Union never were these 100 years (I might go farther) in our own management, and I doubt whether any measures can put them so at present.'[23] This meant that Scottish affairs were at best a side show. Colonial attitudes were routinely exhibited towards Scotland. This was exemplified by the influx of revenue officials sent to Scotland after the union; more dramatically by the action of the Duke of Cumberland after Culloden; and more subtly by the Duke of Newcastle in his official correspondence over the years.

Another underlying reason was that English anxieties or prejudices about Scotland continued long after the union and made the role of the Scottish newcomers to parliament and those who remained in the administration at home difficult. There was a sort of racial prejudice – on both sides, it has to be said. In 1718 the choleric lord advocate, Sir David Dalrymple, wrote of 'an innate presumptuous notion about Englishmen and English laws and a contempt for Scotsmen and the laws there'. The most blatant demonstration was in the overtly racist rabble-rousing of John Wilkes in his defence of 'English liberties' in the 1760s and 70s. In considering Scottish disappointments in political life in the half century after the union, however, it would be incorrect to place too much emphasis on such prejudice. Prejudice though there was, it was not as strong as the pervasive, subtly different colonial attitude and was not the prime factor in holding Scots back in politics at any time in the century. The shared affinities of the English and Scots elites, including increasing links by marriage, diminished it.

When we look at the backgrounds of leading Scottish figures, Bute and his uncles, Argyll and Ilay, it may be discerned that they could hardly have been distinguishable from their English counterparts, although Bute's stay in Scotland in his early childhood certainly gave him some sort of Scottish accent. Each of them was a leader in London society. Scots did not flourish to their full potential at the heart of politics for many decades, but they could thrive in elite activities with links to politics, holding senior offices in the royal households, the army and diplomatic services. For example, at times between 1710 and the 1760s, John, second Duke of Argyll and Lords Orkney, Stair and Home held very high military posts; and Lords Stair, Polwarth and Hyndford and Sir Andrew Mitchell (formerly Tweeddale's undersecretary) were diplomatists of the first rank. The rather indiscriminate association in the English mind of Scots with Jacobitism also took its toll. For example, the secretaries of state, in their concern for the suppression of civil disorder, tended to focus their attention in their Scottish business upon Jacobitism until about the early 1750s. The spasmodic demonising of Argyll and Ilay themselves as Jacobites by their Whig enemies in England and Scotland also tended to associate Scots as a matter of course with the Jacobite menace. It was convenient to besmirch these Highland chiefs with accusations of Jacobitism and perhaps it was half believed. If the alliance of the ultra-Whig Junto and the squadrone in the years after the union had established itself in power, the linking of the Scottish political orthodoxy to Jacobitism would have had much less strength. This is not to deny the real potency of Jacobitism in Scotland outside the political mainstream. It was one of the factors encouraging the trivialisation of Scottish politics. In Scotland a Tory was synonymous with a Jacobite – that is in crude, generalised terms. The case was not quite so extreme in England, whatever people's suspicions about the Tories there.

The imperceptible line between Jacobitism and Toryism in Scotland meant that the Whigs monopolised the country's orthodox politics. In consequence, personal rivalries were the main party or factional issue among the Scottish Whigs. For years after the union, Scottish Whig politics were dominated by the factional rivalry between the adherents of the Argyll family and their inherently weaker rivals, the squadrone. There were also independent Whigs and the local territorial interests and rivalries of great magnates. But the competition for power and for a share of the spoils between the two factions took centre stage until the mid 1740s, when Tweeddale was secretary of state. The feud or, at least, the animosity tottered on into the 1750s. This was signified in the frosty relations of the Dundases of Arniston and the Marchmont family with the third Duke of Argyll (Ilay) in the 50s; and in the dealings of Lord Milton, who looked after the latter's political housekeeping in Scotland and who made no voluntary concessions throughout his career, which ended in the early 1760s, to people with old squadrone links unless they had reformed. But by 1720 the squadrone politicians had lost their cohesion as a group, their comradely spirit, thanks to political disappointment and the failings of their leaders, Montrose and Roxburghe. By that stage, the squadrone was hardly more than a set of people with past ties, being, broadly speaking, sympathetic towards each other only in their animosity towards their opponents.

Taking a step back from that particular dispute and turning to Scottish electoral politics in general, the latter were very subject to baleful influences. In one sense, these trivialised or reduced Scotland's contribution to the national political scene; but in contrast to this, there were also elements in electoral politics that gave the country more of a role than it could otherwise have expected. On the negative side, the root problem was the very small size of the Scottish electorate. The electorate was tiny in comparison with that of England, even allowing for England's much greater population. At the union Scotland was given 45 seats in the House of Commons. Fifteen of these were allocated to the 66 royal burghs. Edinburgh got one seat. The rest were divided into nine districts of five burghs and five districts of four burghs; each district returning a member to Westminster. The burghs were self-electing oligarchies (see Chapter 7), all of them having their own constitutions (the burgh setts). Each council in a district of burghs elected a commissioner to vote at the election of the parliamentary representative. The host burgh (by rota) supplied the presiding officer at the parliamentary election. He had a casting vote in the event of a tie – a most important consideration in the districts of four burghs.[24]

The other 30 Scottish seats in the Commons were allocated to representatives of the counties. Twenty-four of the counties had a single member. The remaining six counties, the smaller ones, were divided into three pairs, the counties in each pair alternating to elect a member. In 1788 there were only 2662 electors enrolled for all the Scottish counties. This small figure includes nominal or fictitious votes created by landowners to increase their political influence, a practice that was becoming more prevalent after the end of the Seven Years' War in 1763, despite the heavy costs involved.[25] To qualify as an elector, a landholder had to be in possession of freehold land over a certain value, either 40s land of old extent in medieval terms, or, as was a prevalent qualification in the eighteenth century, infeftment in freehold land currently rated for taxation purposes at £400 Scots (the Scots pound being equal to a twelfth of the pound sterling). There were a variety of legal subterfuges used to multiply votes without depriving the real freeholders of their land.

'New money' also came into the system. Henry Dundas, a fast rising star on the national scene after becoming the member for
Midlothian in 1774 and lord advocate in 1775, was particularly vexed
by the intervention of the new money of Sir Lawrence Dundas in the
political competition. Sir Lawrence made his fortune as a contractor
for army supplies. Despite these changes, it is concluded that at the
end of the century, Henry Dundas, the political manager of Scotland
on behalf of Pitt, had 'dominated the Scottish electorate for over 20
years'.[26] The rich diversity of corrupt practices that such a small and
therefore manipulable electorate engendered both in the counties and
the burghs need not detain us here. The only comment I would make
in that respect is to note that much of the work of political managers
in getting a satisfactory outcome at elections was done not at the elections themselves (a fair proportion of which were uncontested), but
in the years between elections. Thus Ilay and Milton wasted none of
the opportunities that came their way in filling offices or making recommendations about these in order to build up a national body of
support and create an understanding as to where power lay. The best
example of Dundas's planning was in the northeast of Scotland in the
late 1780s. He was troubled, firstly, by a clash between two government supporters, the territorial magnates Earl Fife (in the Irish
peerage) and the Duke of Gordon, which was leading to the return of
opposition candidates; secondly by the unsure allegiance of the MP
for Banffshire, Fife's son; and lastly, by the hold a leading opposition
figure, William Adam, had on the Elgin burghs. Dundas reconciled
Fife and Gordon, and gave recognition to Fife's ability to carry three
counties on his own. A settlement was arrived at which covered Aberdeenshire, Banffshire, the county of Elgin and the Elgin burghs. In
due course he engineered 'a pattern of alliances' which, after the general election of 1790, almost excluded opponents of the government
from seats in the north and northeast.[27]

   Less effort was put in, at least by Ilay, in looking after the election
of the 16 representative peers. Modest cash payments to lesser peers
could be just what was needed to secure their vote in the ballot. This
was certainly what was done by Ilay. It should not be supposed, however, that his methods were unsophisticated. The Earl of Breadalbane,
who was born in 1696 and succeeded to his title in 1752, wrote from
Edinburgh in January 1771 to his daughter to explain how things
were done by Ilay, Duke Archibald, at the peers' elections, which always took place in Edinburgh. Breadalbane's letter was written after a

contentious by-election:

> As to one of your queries, whether this was the first time of the Min__rs
> writing to the Peers? The custom is very modern. Arch. D of Argyll had the
> nomination, but in a different manner, for some persons here who did his
> dirty work [Milton and his associates] took care to let all the Peers know
> who would be agreeable, and the knowing from whence the authority came
> almost always acquiesced. This was certainly influencing, but it was not
> done in so open a manner. I can not find that any Min__r interfered so
> publicly before the D of G[rafto]n and Ld N[orth] seems to have copied his
> letter from one writt by his Grace.[28]

In 1710 the future Duke Archibald and his elder brother, Duke John,
were altogether more brutal in their handling of the peers' election
(Chapter 3). As for the 1780s, the government abandoned the issuing of the 'king's list' in 1782 and reverted to more discreet methods
than those introduced by Grafton. To conclude the matter of Scottish
electoral politics, it must always be recognised that references to the
success of the two great political managers of the century, Ilay and
Henry Dundas, in exercising control are further examples of the convenient generalisations we have to deal with. In the Commons'
elections there were a great variety of local influences, including competing local magnates and families. Nevertheless, the broad conclusion
remains that during the course of two long spells, Scottish political
initiative was suppressed through the careful exploitation of patronage. The exercise of control was greater in Scotland than in England
because of the very small size of the Scottish electorate.

There is another side to the story, an important one in the shaping
of Scotland's political destiny. There are two points here. The first is
that, as an accidental outcome of the system of management, the Scots
were unintentionally given political clout that could be used against
the ministry of the day. Management normally led to a compliant
body of support in the House of Commons for the administration,
but there were inherent risks. This was seen, for example, at the general election of 1741 when the Argyll family interest was split by Duke
John's defection from the government side, and contributed to
Walpole's downfall. There was a less dramatic example in the summer of 1755 when Newcastle, the first lord of the treasury – who had
been aiming to circumvent Argyll in Scottish affairs – found himself
with the support of only three friends among the 45 Scottish MPs and

had to reach a hasty accommodation with the Duke. In early 1782 there was another case, at a time when the prime minister Lord North was scraping along with shrinking majorities. Dundas, who had much influence with the government's Scottish members (but was not yet the manager for Scotland), asked for the dismissal of Lord George Germain, the secretary of state for the colonies, over the government's American policy. North did not act until Dundas had withdrawn from the House threatening not to return as long as Germain remained in office. North capitulated and dismissed Germain, fearing that he would lose the Scottish votes. The government would, in short, have collapsed if North had not acceded to Dundas's demand.[29]

The second point is that the block of support created by the great managers Ilay and Henry Dundas brought stability to the scene. The obverse was mayhem in the general election of 1768 when Scotland was managerless.[30] The work of Henry Dundas, who was Scottish manager briefly on behalf of Lord Shelburne in 1782–83 and from the end of 1783 under Pitt, was particularly advantageous in this regard, in that he painstakingly built up regional alliances in Scotland and gained the consent of a large section of the landed interest, 'whose aspirations he understood and advanced'.[31] Political stability, particularly one of such an intrisically 'benevolent' nature had benefits for Scottish society. During the Walpole era, a long period of relative stability helped the Scots towards political acceptance. At the end of the century, stability worked with other political and social developments to help establish the Scots as full partners in the United Kingdom.

The first Scot to reach great prominence within the English political status quo was Bute. His spectacular rise to power came with the accession of George III in 1760. Bute, the King's favourite, was first lord of the treasury in 1762 to 1763. His impact on the course of the politics of Scotland was only to set back their progress towards fuller integration with those of England. Although general detestation of Bute in England arose from his being advanced to power simply on the basis of his friendship with the King, it was displayed in the form of ribald references to his Scotchness. This was a bit of an aberration in the political development of the time. Before Bute came on the scene there were signs of greater tolerance among English politicians, a change in old attitudes towards their northern neighbours. By the late 1750s the Jacobite threat had run its course, so that Scotland itself was less of a problem for England. Scotland was also less of a client state, contributing a net surplus to the public revenues. The real watershed came at this time, not with Bute, but with the outbreak of the Seven Years' War in 1756. Scots were zealously British in supporting the national cause. And Argyll was at last in full favour at court, through the gratitude of George II for a valuable contribution to the war effort in helping to raise Scottish troops. Matters were helped by the eclipse of the Duke of Cumberland after the defeat at the Battle of Hastenbeck in 1757, and by his diplomatic failure at the peace conference that followed. He had been the most dangerous enemy of Scotland and, more specifically, of the Argyll family.

The old rivalries among the Scottish Whigs and between the old warhorses, Newcastle and the third Duke of Argyll, had already almost run their course when the latter died in 1761, and the factional rivalries expired in 1763 with the retirement of Lord Milton. Scottish politics were beginning to mature. Meanwhile there was accelerating integration of Scots into English society. They were at last beginning to be successful in politics. This was as much because of their abilities as their English connections. The earliest example of this new success was in the career of Lord Dupplin, MP for Cambridge, grandson of Lord Oxford. Dupplin was Newcastle's adviser on electoral matters for the whole country in the mid 1750s and also on treasury business for some years. Another success was William Murray, a younger son of the fourth Viscount of Stormont. Murray was a meritocrat, a man of business first and an aristocrat second. He was raised from his infancy in England. In 1731 he became a member of the English bar. In 1756 he became lord chief justice of the King's Bench and received a British peerage (Mansfield). He also became a member of the cabinet and was chancellor of the exchequer for a few months in 1757. His nephew, David Murray, Lord Stormont, was like him educated at Westminster School and Christ Church College, Oxford. After a successful diplomatic career, he held office as the secretary for the northern department in 1779–82. Alexander Wedderburn, son of an undistinguished Scottish judge, was a young Scottish lawyer who became a member of the English bar and then an MP in England, initially for Richmond in Yorkshire. His political career in government and opposition culminated in his appointment as lord chancellor in the administration of the younger Pitt in 1793. Mansfield and Wedderburn were mocked because of their Anglified accents, but they were still successful men.

Again, Scots were as much involved as were the English in responding to the big political challenges at the end of the century. At this time Henry Dundas, as home secretary, was at the centre of the reaction of the British political classes to the radicalism of the 1790s. Among those opposing him, it may be added, was the Scot William Adam, who was manager of the opposition Whigs' machine. But in the creation of a truly British society, Dundas was the greatest representative of change. It was his achievement to break down the portals of the English establishment. This he did as a member for Scottish constituencies (apart from a brief spell in 1782 as MP for Newtown, Isle of Wight, a temporary measure), without the political advantages of an English education or close English family connections. He reached the heights of influence, not merely in the offices of home secretary and secretary for war, but as William Pitt's close associate in government in the 1780s and 1790s. For a time he shared this role with William Grenville (Lord Grenville, 1790) and then he took it on alone.

Dundas is often remembered in Scotland not for those deeds, but, through the writing of Alexander Carlyle, for his effectiveness in the narrow area of political management, ranking with Ilay as one of the two great managers of Scottish politics in the eighteenth century. Dundas's achievement was altogether different in nature, however, perhaps helped by the changes in the political climate at the end of the century. He used his influence in Scotland to assist his British political ambitions, whereas Ilay was baulked in his attempts and settled for less. In this Ilay represented the old political order, the years of suppression of the Scottish political spirit. Dundas represented a new order in which Scots could participate in British politics as true partners.[32]

3

THE STRUGGLE FOR CONTROL, 1707–25

The Early Years

In *The English Ministers and Scotland, 1707-1727*, Patrick Riley describes the years of great political complexity immediately after the union, and charts important changes and developments in relationships between the two countries and their politicians. This chapter draws upon his immense work, while taking a different emphasis and not quite so caustic a view of politicians' motives. In dealing with the period up to 1725, the approach here is to focus, but not exclusively, on the activities of John, second Duke of Argyll, and his brother, Lord Ilay, and on their political relationships with the squadrone, the Junto, the Duke of Marlborough, Lord Oxford and Walpole. Their relations with Marlborough and his friends were particularly important influences on the course of Scottish politics up to the early 1720s. The brothers do not provide the whole key to the period, but there was very little happening that did not involve or relate to them in some way. Their exploits, their failure and, ultimately, their success take us into the heart of British politics, showing how the politics of Scotland and England were entwined. Moreover, after the decline of Queensberry, the Argyll family interest in Scotland was the most powerful force in orthodox, essentially Whig, Scottish politics – in other words, outside the alternative world of Jacobitism.

However, as David Hayton observes, Argyll's influence was at a nadir in 1708. Through Ilay's painstaking efforts in the recruitment of new clients, it gradually recovered. Under Ilay's guidance, says Hayton, 'the Argyll interest grew silently and inexorably, like a pike in a tank of goldfish.'[1] As long as successive administrations in London gave priority to keeping that power in check rather than harnessing it, the Scottish political scene would be turbulent, as it was until 1725. The negative attitude in London towards Argyll was very understandable given that working with the ungovernable Duke could be painful. He also made enemies in England who were much more powerful than himself, which contributed to damaging his career and Ilay's. However, once Walpole decided, from at least the early 1720s, on the priority of harnessing Argyll's strength in Scotland to bolster his own parliamentary interest and accepted that the need to keep the Duke in check was secondary, an era of political stability for Scotland was at hand.

The representatives sent from Scotland to sit in the first British parliament before a general election took place in 1708 were elected in the last parliament of Scotland. Their support for the union was thereby ensured. London became the centre of Scottish politics. Even before the union took place, there had been jockeying for position – in both England and Scotland – in anticipation of the change. With union achieved, competition quickly broke out. This did much to influence the important events which were to follow, bringing about the abolition of the Scottish Privy Council within a year. Matters of principle were also at stake and have to be added to the equation, hard though it can be at times to measure their impact given the strength of personal and factional divisions. The Scottish court interest which did so much to further the cause of union in alliance with the squadrone was a temporary coalition, dominated as it was by Queensberry, Argyll, Mar and Seafield, men with their own ambitions. It quickly lost its cohesion, with Mar, Argyll and Ilay, who were to come to the fore, unsympathetic towards Queensberry and looking for change.

The squadrone, now zealously and overtly Whig in a newly formed alliance with the English Junto – a group of zealous and ambitious Whig lords – were themselves deeply fearful of the undue arrogation of power by Queensberry and the court group. And old animosities remained between the squadrone and Argyll: this rivalry became the most significant factor in the longer term. In looking towards the future development of Scottish politics, it is convenient to pass by some features that were important at the time; the Treason Act of 1708 for example, which caused much irritation by making the Scots conform to the English treason law; and, again, the disappointment and vexation of Scottish peers about limitations that were placed on them. It is also convenient to pass by some of the pre-union grandees, such as Hamilton, Seafield, Loudoun and Annandale, as yesterday's men, although each in his own way had a transitory impact; as when the maverick Hamilton (killed in a duel in Hyde Park in 1712) allied with the squadrone in the 1708 peers' election; and when Seafield led calls for the abolition of the union in 1713, the year in which his office of lord chancellor of Scotland was also briefly revived by Lord Oxford.

The antecedents of the animosity between the squadrone and the Campbell brothers, Argyll and Ilay, apart from that arising from the competition for power, came out of Scotland's factional past. In the more recent past, the Argyll family had grievances against three of the squadrone families, Tweeddale, Marchmont and Montrose, relating to the ninth Earl of Argyll's expedition in support of Monmouth in 1685 and the Earl's execution in that year. Traditional feuds were insignificant, however, compared with a great cause of tension between Argyll and the squadrone – the clash of the Montrose and Argyll electoral interests. This was fierce in the Glasgow burghs and in Dunbartonshire.[2] Montrose spent part of his childhood in Glasgow, where his mother had a dower house, and he went to university there. He was a man to whom the authorities in the town and university deferred, much to the irritation of Argyll, for whom Glasgow was an obviously important political target. The competing electoral interests of the two men also spread much further afield. Montrose's seat was at Buchanan House in Stirlingshire on the east side of Loch Lomond, where his estate stretched into Perthshire. The extent of his estates and the scope for conflict had increased dramatically in 1704, when – through the determination of his henchman, Mungo Graeme of Gorthie, and almost despite himself – Montrose brought off a major coup by buying the greater part of the lands and rights of the dukedom of Lennox, also embracing the earldoms of Darnley and Tarbolton. He purchased the Lennox estates for £20 000 sterling from Sir David Hamilton, the Queen's physician. Hamilton had, just previously, received a disposition of them from Frances, Lady Lanesborough, in a rather obscure arrangement involving debts, she having the estates from Charles II's natural son, the Duke of Richmond and Lennox.[3]

At that time, it may be noted, the Argyll family could not compete for this purchase – even if they had been allowed to do so. They were in poor financial circumstances. This may be attributed to the previous forfeiture of their estates, restored to them upon the accession of William and Mary, and the improvidence of the first Duke (died 1703). At the union Montrose's interests included lands in Stirlingshire, Perthshire, Dunbartonshire, Renfrewshire and Ayrshire, and some interest in the barony of Glasgow. His presence in Glasgow remained modest because the regality of Glasgow, which had been retained by the Duke of Richmond and Lennox, was not included in the sale. The Queen, as feudal superior, had swithered in agreeing to Montrose's acquisition of the Lennox estates. In her caution, she will have been advised by Queensberry (much though she disliked him), who claimed to have spoken to her repeatedly for a decision in Montrose's favour, and by Godolphin. This major transfer of ownership was politically and socially sensitive. She stipulated, first, that rights respecting Dumbarton Castle should revert to the crown and, second, that the Lennox vassals should be given the chance to buy their superiorities from Montrose. Superiorities had, of course, electoral importance in qualifying their holders – freeholders – to vote. Mungo Graeme was not too downhearted by the stipulation about them, advising Montrose that: 'I'm sure ye cannot but see that a great many will still remain in your own hands, and with good manadgement ye may gett a great part of those ye most incline for . . . .'[4]

Montrose does not seem to have exploited the political potential of his estates to the full, but there was still plenty of scope for conflict between him and Argyll. In this there was something almost intangible, the challenge to Argyll's leadership of southwest Highland society posed by the presence of Montrose there. As a source of conflict, this was symbolised in a relatively trivial way by Argyll's vexatious protection of Rob Roy Macgregor, whose depredations on Montrose's Buchanan estate lasted for many years. There was also an affront to Argyll in the heart of his own domains. In 1684 Montrose's father, as creditor of the deceased Marquis of Argyll, was granted lands in Cowal out of the Argyll estates forfeited to the crown. To the proud Duke John and his resolute mother, the dowager Duchess Elizabeth, this would have been barely tolerable.

The competition between the squadrone and Argyll was all the more powerful because of the English connections and rivalries affecting it. The squadrone and the Junto became natural allies, determined to further the Whig cause and their own careers. They were closely associated in the years following the union. Symbolising the attachment was the marriage in 1708 of one of the squadrone's leaders, Roxburghe, into the family of one of the Junto lords, Halifax, and the employment of Robert Pringle, cousin of the squadrone Earl of Marchmont, as the Earl of Sunderland's secretary. The Junto themselves were in an uneasy coalition with the Godolphin ministry which had Tory antecedents. The Queen found it difficult to stomach the Whiggery of the Junto – perhaps most of all their attitude to the Church of England – but she and the duumvirs in power, Godolphin and the Duke of Marlborough, needed their support to prosecute the war, that is the War of the Spanish Succession, at a time when neither the Tories nor the Whigs had a clear majority. In return the Junto were pressing for a greater share of ministerial posts. The first reluctant concession to them had been Sunderland's appointment as secretary for the southern department in December 1706. Further appointments followed, but the Junto aim was power for themselves, whereas Godolphin would have liked to do without them. For the squadrone, the difficulty was that Godolphin showed no sign of placing Scottish affairs in their hands, despite their alliance with his ministerial partners in the Junto. He was content to leave matters well alone and let the Queensberry-led court group continue to manage Scotland as they did before the union. Equally, Godolphin did not want to hand the Scottish management over to the Junto via the squadrone. It was in the interest of the squadrone therefore to conspire with the Junto to undermine Godolphin and the Scottish court group.

For Argyll and Ilay, there were other problems. They were contemptuous of the squadrone and they were jealous of Queensberry; but, to make matters worse, Argyll had by this time conceived a terrible hatred for his commanding officer, Marlborough, commander of the army in the war with France. This hatred was to reach its apogee in 1710 and had an impact for years to come. In political terms the split was all the more damaging because Sunderland, leader of the Junto, was Marlborough's son-in-law, even though not on the best of terms. Moreover, Marlborough's closest associate, the Irishman William Cadogan, was to become a powerful political figure within a few years and was Argyll's hated rival in their ambitions for advancement in the army. There was utter loathing on both sides. In total, the predicament of Argyll and Ilay, certainly in 1708 to 1710, was that their relations with Queensberry were not good and he was in any case becoming a spent force; their relations with the Godolphin-Marlborough duumvirate were damaged irretrievably; they could not ally with the

Junto, because of the Junto-squadrone combination; they could not supplant the squadrone in the Junto's affections because Sunderland headed the Junto; and the Junto dominated Whig politics at the time. With the benefit of hindsight, it is clear that if ever Argyll and Ilay were to flourish politically in the post-union political settlement, it could only be when the Junto-Marlborough influence in the Whig party had gone or been dissipated (although Marlborough, who died in 1722, was not himself a Whig) or if they were to ally with the Tories. For the moment, the brothers were ambitious – they had potentially the most powerful interest in Scotland yet they seemed impotent. At least they had youth on their side, being still in their twenties in 1707.

Immediately after the union, the initiative lay with the squadrone and the Junto. They started making their plans to undermine the authority of the court group in Scotland by getting the Scottish Privy Council abolished. The Privy Council's fate had been left an open question at the union. The squadrone and Junto were determined that it should go. A bill was introduced to abolish it and, in its place, to increase the powers of the justices of the peace in Scotland, who were to deal with matters of public order over which the Council had authority. With Tory support and against the wishes of Godolphin and the court group, the bill became law in February 1708. The squadrone had made their plans public in December 1707, but there is a hint that they may have been in discussions about them in late summer.

In establishing motives, *A History of Great Britain,* written by one Alexander Cunningham, is valuable. The role of this shadowy figure (son of a minister of the parish of Ettrick) in events at the time of the union would merit research. A Whig zealot who was among those accompanying William of Orange to England in 1688, he is easily confused with a great chess master and classical scholar of the same name (alas, I have been guilty of this myself). Cunningham was a political fixer who helped advise the Junto on Scottish matters and he eased their communications with the squadrone, as a few letters from him to Montrose help to suggest. By his own account, he was involved in planning the Privy Council's demise. He had been a travelling tutor to young gentlemen in Europe, including the future Duke of Argyll (it seems until about April 1698); indeed, in his *History,* he continued to scold Argyll for his wrong-headed ways. In 1701 Cunningham was employed by King William on a commercial mission to Paris, corresponding with the Reverend William Carstares, the King's one-time Scottish adviser, about this. Cunningham was to become British representative in Venice in 1715.

The real sources of his influence were twofold. First, he was friendly with the future essayist, Joseph Addison, another traveller in Europe at the beginning of the century. They visited Hanover together on a mission in 1703. Addison was, it need hardly be said, a true-blue Whig, a member of the Kit-Cat Club – founded by the leading Whigs of the day – and was employed during the events of 1707 and 1708 as undersecretary to Sunderland. In 1707 Cunningham arranged to receive mail under Addison's cover at Sunderland's office. Second, Cunningham scoured Europe for rare books and manuscripts on behalf of great collectors, certainly Harley, Sunderland and Lord Somers (another Junto leader), although when he started doing this is uncertain. When in pursuit of treasures, the political persuasions of Cunningham and these ruthless enthusiasts were set at naught. He was able to deal with leading politicians from either side of the great divide with some familiarity, just as Addison could. Cunningham's political credentials are stressed by the translator of his history, which was written in Latin. Cunningham called Whigs *moderati* and Tories *rigidi*. He was angry that Godolphin, in settling the government of Scotland after the union, 'neither consulted Sommers, Halifax, Montrose, Roxburgh, nor anybody else, but Queensberry, Seafield, Marr, and a few of his creatures'.

While referring to himself modestly – 'a certain private gentleman of the Whig party' – he managed to blow his own trumpet. Even allowing for his exaggeration, motives behind the determination to the abolish the Privy Council are espied, the usual mixture of principle and short-term factionalism; an appeal to Whig values, a desire to make the union more complete, and to remove the remnants of the arbitrary and corrupt pre-union regime by abolishing the Privy Council, the power base in Scotland of the court group. Cunningham says that he himself:

> began to contrive how to get the privy council of Scotland abolished, of which the Duke of Queensberry was president, and this remnant of the ancient tyranny removed. The next summer, therefore [1707], he framed a combination of some of the chief of the Scots, and all those who were unacceptable, disgusted and incensed against the Queensberry faction.

He sought to have:

> all the relics of tyranny in Scotland removed, and the council abolished by
> the parliament; for he had nothing else in view but the public liberty.[5]

In early 1708 the Junto's push for power continued. The politics of
the time were shaped by the war on the Continent. Defeat at the Battle of Alamanza in Spain in the previous summer had led to
recriminations at home. There was also disagreement between Junto
and the Tories on the need for peace, the Junto taking a hard line in
not agreeing to accept any peace which left Spain in the hands of
Louis XIV's grandson. This entailed the continuing vigorous prosecution of war against France. Godolphin went with the Junto on this.
The moderate Tory secretary for the northern department, Harley,
was forced out of office and other Tories followed. The Whigs appeared to have a grip on government when they achieved a clear
majority in the House of Commons at the general election in May
1708. Riley assesses that the squadrone contributed nine members.[6]
However the Scottish aims of the Junto and squadrone were not realised. The Junto's ambition to undermine Godolphin by replacing
Queensberry with the squadrone was not achieved. In particular, there
had been misplaced Junto-squadrone hopes of success in the election
of the 16 representative peers, in which the Junto and squadrone
operated a pact with the Duke of Hamilton and other noble suspect-
ed-Jacobites arrested in 1708 after the invasion attempt of that year.
Under the pact, the suspects were released in exchange for their votes.
A withering contemporary comment on the squadrone's cynical part
in this was that: 'they boasted of their alliance with the Whig lords in
England, they proclaimed their alliance with the Jacobite nobility in
Scotland.'[7]

Before the election Halifax injected a note of realism, confiding to
Montrose that 'we have done our best to make your elections good'
and that if defeated: 'we will be so far from giving up the glorious
cause we have undertaken, of uniting Britain upon a solid and national interest, and freeing both parts of the kingdom from being
enslaved from the corruption of the other.'[8] These admirable hopes
were dashed. The Scottish court group obtained majorities in the elections to the Lords and Commons; and Godolphin continued his
support for Queensberry. The post of third secretary of Great Britain
was created for Queensberry early in 1709, while other people, both

the squadrone and court supporters, had to be content with lesser appointments.

For Scottish politicians the period from 1708 to 1714, when Queen Anne died, was marked not so much by the desultory term of office of the weakening Queensberry, who died in 1711, as by the effects of war and unsatisfactory peace on the politics of Great Britain as a whole. This led to the eclipse of the Whig interest, which put the squadrone's prospects on hold. It also allowed the re-emergence of Harley (Earl of Oxford from May 1711). This gave brief opportunities to Mar and the Jacobites – not completely the same thing at this time. It also gave Argyll and Ilay opportunities; but it ended in their bitter disappointment: first, because Harley's approach to politics, his moderation, in Scotland as in England did not allow for the dominance of individuals or factions; second, because of wider political and diplomatic considerations; and third, because of Argyll's intemperance. The outcome was that the brothers were reduced to bit parts, a dangerous state of affairs given their ambitions.

Shortly after the election in 1708, Marlborough defeated the French at Oudenarde, with relatively few casualties. There followed the long siege of Lille which concluded successfully, but with terrible casualties. The campaign carried on into the severe winter of 1708–9, when the strategically important towns of Ghent and Bruges were recaptured from the French. France sued for peace. Optimism was dashed, however, at the peace conference in The Hague in the spring of 1709, when the French surprised Marlborough by rejecting the allies' extreme demands. Seemingly endless war resumed; expenditure on it grew; compulsory recruitment continued apace; and the national mood changed. Disintegration was in the air. Despondency ruled at court. When Sir John Clerk of Penicuik visited Kensington Palace in the previous year, he was introduced to the Queen, the 'Arbitrix of peace and war in Europe' in her lonely court: 'The poor Lady, as I saw her twice before, was again under a severe fit of the Gout, ill dressed, blotted in her countenance, and surrounded with plaisters, cataplasims, and dirty-like rags.'[9] Now her dismay was complete. She accepted continuing war with a leaden heart and she hated the Junto, apart from a softening in her attitude towards Somers. At the same time relations between her and Sarah, Duchess of Marlborough, had broken down. Sarah, her groom of the stole, harangued and insulted her. Meanwhile, Harley worked his way into the Queen's favour and set about undermining the ministry. In late summer came the bloodshed of

Malplaquet, claimed as a victory. In the winter of 1709–10 came food shortages, and rising prices in London and other towns, after a poor harvest caused by the previous long, harsh winter. War weariness and a mood of unrest set in with a vengeance.

It was the time for Argyll to make his bid. Among his personal motives, his ambitions and those of his brother to have the management of Scotland were probably not central. Cutting a grand figure on the British national stage and ambitions in the army were probably of more immediate interest to the Duke. In this respect, it is noteworthy that the command he was given in Spain in 1710 was said to be worth some £20 000 a year, exceeding the whole Scottish civil list. Yet Scotland was the source of his influence; it was never far from his mind; and hanging on grimly in his wake was Ilay, whose Scottish ambitions were undoubted. When Argyll returned home to London at the end of the 1709 campaign, he was leader of a group of discontented officers, notably Earl Rivers, and the Earl of Orrery who was Argyll and Ilay's particular friend (although later a Jacobite) and also on good terms at this time with Harley. This group, encouraged by Harley, vilified Marlborough. Argyll, contributing his mite to destabilising the ministry and sitting in the Lords as the Earl of Greenwich in the English peerage, launched an attack on the captain-general in the House, accusing him of mismanagement and the squandering of life at Malplaquet. This was a horrifying battle between the allies and the French. Argyll's brigade is known to have sustained heavy losses. Argyll and his associates have been dismissed with contempt by Winston Churchill and other Marlborough biographers, but it is impossible to say how far personal slights and thwarted ambitions influenced things.

Argyll certainly had petty personal motives going back to at least 1708, and it is believed he was upset with the price Marlborough made him pay for a regiment for Ilay in 1709 to enable the latter to resume a modest military career. Argyll's selfish political motives were even stronger. He continued to further these in February–March 1710 at the House of Lords impeachment proceedings of Dr Henry Sacheverell, against a background of anti-Whig riots. A sermon at St Paul's in the previous November by this cleric, attacking the Whig-dominated ministry and the principle of the Hanoverian succession, was to provide the catalyst for political change. The folly of the ministry in deciding to impeach him was the flashpoint. In the course of the trial a 'middle party', positioned between the Junto and the high Tories, began to assert itself. It consisted of the Duke of Shrewsbury, the

Duke of Somerset and Argyll.

It was in Argyll's interest that the Junto prosecution should be defeated; but, as head of a family recognised in Scotland as protectors of Protestantism and presbytery, he could not vote for the Tory parson's acquittal. He voted therefore for a light sentence which would amount to a defeat for the Whigs. Harley's emissary, Orrery, reported to Harley before the vote that Argyll thought: 'an absolute acquittal would rather tend to promote a high Tory scheme than to ruin the interest of the Junto; besides he's afraid he should prejudice his interest in Scotland by it. However, he thinks he may fairly oppose any excessive punishment that shall be proposed . . ..'[10] Upon being found guilty Sacheverell was merely sentenced to be banned from preaching for three years. Public rejoicing at this snub signalled the imminent demise of the ministry. In June Sunderland was dismissed by the Queen, to be followed by Godolphin two months later. Harley succeeded Godolphin as head of the ministry, initially in the post of chancellor of the exchequer and in due course as lord treasurer. Parliament was dissolved by the Queen in September and a general election was called.

At last Argyll and Ilay were given a leading role in the political management of Scotland, despite some vacillating by Harley. But soon they were to be thwarted in their ambitions. These did not fit in with Harley's requirements. In England his policy of a political balance came under stress even before the general election, with the resignation, for example, of the moderate Whig secretary for the northern department, Henry Boyle, and his replacement by the ambitious high Tory, Henry St John (Viscount Bolingbroke, 1712). These were early signs not of moderation, but of Tory domination of the ministry and of Harley's need to compete with St John to retain control. In the political management, such as it was, of Scotland under Harley, a fundamental weakness in the quest for balance and moderation was the failure to embrace the political realities. These were that the orthodoxy in church and state was Whig and that Argyll's political interest was an important presence there. To make matters worse, another important group, the squadrone, could not work with Harley; while the previous ministry's secretary of state, Queensberry, was retained so as not to alienate his group, but was pretty well ignored and was not replaced until some time after his death in 1711. In other words, Harley diverted Scottish politics from their natural course. Partly by choice, he relied too much on Scottish Tories – Jacobite sympathisers – who did not represent the political status quo there and, in his fear of great men and faction in

Scotland, he depended on one of the English barons of the exchequer who had been implanted in Scotland, John Scrope, as his right-hand-man in Scottish affairs.

In a sense, Harley's system, which has been looked at in detail by Riley, was a sort of intrusion imposed upon Scotland just a few years after the union. It was certainly not the sort of partnership between England and Scotland discerned in the agreement between the Junto and the squadrone in the early days. Even the appointment of Mar as secretary of state in September 1713 was not done primarily to help Scotland. It was partly in response to the inability of Oxford, as Harley had become, to cope with the workload. It was in the main, however, as Riley explains, a move designed by Oxford to counteract Bolingbroke's ambition to manage Scotland through his own office as secretary of state.[11] Bolingbroke also changed from being secretary for the north to being that for the south around the same time. Mar was recognised as a weak secretary, lacking a strong power base in Scotland and undermined by his Jacobite leanings, his talent as a quietly competent man of business notwithstanding. To understand the particular choice of Mar as secretary, it should be understood that he was a friend of Harley's, firmly in his camp, and that they had a family connection through the marriage of Harley's daughter, Abigail, to Mar's brother-in-law, Lord Dupplin, in 1709.[12]

The general elections of 1710 and 1713 illustrate the ultimate fate of Argyll and Ilay under Harley. In October 1710 Ilay and Mar proceeded to Scotland, where they were joined by Argyll, recalled from army duty in Flanders, to manage electoral business for Harley. They were evidently concerned with the peers' election, in particular. There were limits on what they could do in the elections to the Commons – and, in fact, the outcome of these in Scotland was a mixed one from the ministry's point of view. This was because the recent change from a Whig ministry to one with a Tory bias did not permit long-term concerted planning before the election. Moreover, Harley had delayed in giving the managers their instructions. Ilay, using Orrery as his intermediary, had warned Harley that it would not be possible to arrange matters as well as they would have been, 'if proper measures had been taken in time'. Harley's problem was that he was assailed by different interests, a recipe for chaos. For example, Ilay stressed that neither he – Ilay – nor Mar could support any plan which involved working with the squadrone. Then there were representations from Lord Dupplin and the latter's father, Lord Kinnoull, and from their equally dubious Tory associate, the Duke of Atholl. Furthermore, the Duke of Hamilton had to be engaged, but Ilay was not happy that Hamilton's brother, the soldier Orkney, was then on good terms with Marlborough.

Therefore, even before the peers' election held in Edinburgh – in which voters could be dragooned for fear of losing their posts or encouraged by hope of posts and other rewards, and in which the managers could use the proxy votes of absentees loyal to the ministry – the managers had difficulties. The squadrone lords absented themselves, which helped, but there was still disagreement among the peers about a court list of candidates. The list suffered some adjustment in consequence. Queensberry remained in London and did not have a significant role, but his comrade, the Earl of Glasgow, was among those vexed not to be included in the list, though he voted for it, presumably rather than risk his sinecure as lord clerk register. There were doubts about the authority of the managers and unease about Jacobites being included in the list. No matter what the shambles, however, a key feature was the participation of Argyll and Ilay in such management as there was. Daniel Defoe, acting as Harley's agent or informant in Scotland, was incensed by their behaviour. In November, when the elections were concluded, he sent a coded message to Harley complaining about Argyll, Ilay and Mar. They dragooned the peers 'with menaces and contempt' and 'declared openly the qualification of those to be chosen' was to be 'their agreeing to impeach Godolphin and Marlborough'. In other words, those – including Queensberry's clique and the squadrone – who supported the previous administration in its last days were excluded. Defoe later declared that Argyll: 'destroyed the very appearance of liberty in producing a list, and openly telling the Peers, the Queen would have these men chosen.'[13]

How things changed by the time of the next general election, in 1713. Then it was not Mar, Ilay and Argyll who went to Scotland in the autumn to manage things on Oxford's behalf. It was Mar and the Earl of Findlater – that is Seafield, who had succeeded to his father's title. The authority of Mar and Findlater in the management was all the stronger in that Mar was by then secretary of state, and Findlater's old post as lord chancellor of Scotland had been revived. Riley observes that Findlater was made chancellor to prevent the Scottish courts, whose judges included old Whigs appointed in William's reign, from harrying supporters of the ministry. The post was done away with finally on George I's accession. As in 1710 the election of peers produced a good result; whereas in the Commons' election, the ministry had to take the lesser share of the spoils in the face of the success of independent Whigs and the Argyll interest and the squadrone. Argyll and Ilay were again in opposition, Ilay being so out of favour that he was excluded from the peers' list (whereas Argyll's English peerage made him a permanent member of the Lords). Kinnoull, fearing their innate strength in Scotland, had warned Oxford that: 'the turning out of these two brothers is so necessary for making a right election in Scotland, for I acknowledge I think it impossible to make a right election if they are not turned out of all you can take from them.'[14] This was the only time Ilay was not selected for the House of Lords between the union and his death in 1761. Before the peers' election in Edinburgh: 'all the squadrone came to town, as did the Earl of Ilay and the Duke of Argyll's friends.' There was even short-lived talk of a compact between these two factions; but the case was hopeless and they absented themselves from the election.

In the withdrawal of both the main Whig groups lies a clue to part of their problem. Despite Oxford's best intentions not to let the Scottish Tories dominate under his regime, the Tories did do so, while never getting all they would have wished. Also, the plans of Oxford and Bolingbroke in pursuit of peace with France had involved secret overtures to the Pretender about his succeeding to the throne after the Queen's death provided he would change his religion. Oxford and Bolingbroke were not Jacobites in a true sense – they later also made overtures to the house of Hanover – but the Whig principles of the squadrone and Argyll were a threat to the two leaders of the ministry. Again, Argyll and Ilay were too powerful in Scotland for Oxford's taste. Ilay, for his help in managing the 1710 election, got only the post of lord justice general. He had hoped to be secretary of state. He and his brother, having risked their reputations in Whig, Presbyterian Scotland by supporting Oxford and working with Mar, expected their due reward. In November 1712, ground down by disappointment, Ilay addressed Oxford in the bluntest terms: 'we were to be branded with the odious character of having forsook our principles and abandoned the interests of the Protestant Succession, without so much as mitigating the rage and malice which the enemies to it have preserved against us now to the third generation.'[15]

Over the months he became increasingly aware that Mar, who was now commonly recognised as a Jacobite, was to be made secretary.

Ilay warned Oxford in July 1713 that: 'It will be our peculiar misfortune that your Lordship cannot ease yourself of the affairs of Scotland, without leaving us under a greater load of troubles than we have yet felt.'[16] Argyll and Ilay were also too troublesome to Oxford in English politics. In Oxford's view a combination against him – of 'Dukes of Shrewsbury, Argyll; Earls Orrery, Ilay, Anglesey; Bolingbroke; Hanmer, etc.' – was formed in the last session of parliament before the 1713 election. Argyll's personality was another problem. Orrery beseeched Oxford in 1711 to make allowance:

> All his faults I think proceed from his temper . . . the openness of his nature requires perhaps that he should be treated by all his friends with as little reservedness as the good of the public affairs will allow, and that his excellent qualities as well as considerable interest deserve some indulgence I hope for his frailties.[17]

Oxford hit upon the fine idea in that year of packing Argyll off out of harm's way to Spain as ambassador and commander-in-chief: as Mungo Graeme remarked about Argyll's posting: 'some people may desire to have him at a distance.'[18] Oxford tried a similar ploy in 1712 with Ilay, tempting him with a post in Turkey, which his lordship did not choose to accept. For Argyll there was the attraction of not having to work with Marlborough in the Netherlands. But Trevelyan notes that Argyll soon discovered he had been sent to Spain on a fool's errand. As he was not expected to wage war – at a time when the ministry were seeking peace in Europe – he was not given the means to do so. He bombarded the ministers with letters of complaint. The nub of the problem, as he wrote to the Queen, was that: 'to make an army serve without pay is what I am sure I can not do.'[19] In 1712 he took the remnant of his bedraggled army to Minorca, on his next posting as governor there. His sense of outrage in these years set him against the ministry, while in ruling circles his reputation for ungovernability grew.

Against this background of disenchantment, Argyll and Ilay participated in the most curious political incident to affect Scotland since the union. In June 1713 Findlater moved in the House of Lords for leave to introduce a bill for the repeal of the act of union. The motion, predominantly supported by Scottish members and English Whigs, was rejected by four votes. The Scots were at fever pitch at this time after a vote in the Commons to apply the malt tax in Scotland –

and to apply it at the same rate as levied on English malt, despite the superior quality of the English product. This was not only considered unjust, but was technically a breach of the treaty of union, which had stipulated that there would be no imposition upon malt in Scotland 'during this present war'. Riley points out that the Tory country gentlemen had voted to extend the tax to Scotland as a way of getting Scottish support to have the tax abolished in the following session.[20] In fact there was no serious attempt to collect the tax in Scotland and the plan of the Tory gentlemen did not succeed.

Without taking into account personal disappointments, it is hard to explain the motives of the likes of Argyll and Ilay. Ilay was reported as having: 'insisted very violently upon the necessety of prosecuting the desolutione, be the consequences what will'.[21] It is also hard to believe that Argyll and Ilay, and Whigs such as Sunderland and Somers, were really serious in their intention beyond a wish, for tactical reasons, to discomfit the ministry and, as Trevelyan suggests, to curry favour in Scotland before the general election.[22] At the general election after that one, following the accession of George I, the squadrone suspected that Ilay was up to a rather similar trick when a rumour was encouraged that he was behind a petition against the union. The only beneficiaries of actual dissolution in 1713 could have been Jacobites.

With the death of Queen Anne in 1714, the whole political climate changed. There had been fears that Jacobite influences at court, when Bolingbroke was briefly in the ascendant following the dismissal of Oxford, would stop the Hanoverian succession. Traditionally, it has been thought that when the Queen lay on her deathbed, Somerset and Argyll, who had by that time been dismissed from all his offices, burst unauthorised into a meeting of the Privy Council and scuppered a conspiracy that was being hatched there. In fact, there was no such intrusion. A delegation from the Council, including Bolingbroke, went to the Queen and made a recommendation. She gave her assent to the appointment of the moderate Whig, Shrewsbury, as lord treasurer, thereby ensuring a quiet Hanoverian succession. It was after Shrewsbury's appointment that Somerset and Argyll visited the council.[23]

The Rise and Fall of the Squadrone

Upon the proclamation of George I, the great period of Whig domination began in England and Scotland. The time of real opportunity seemed to have come at last for Argyll and his friends. Ilay, with his inimitable sense of the proprieties, hoped, 'that we shall soon have it in our power to do duty in justice both to our friends and our enemies'.[24] His mother, the dowager Duchess Elizabeth, organised a splendid ball at Holyrood, reported Atholl's informant, 'where she herselfe danced a reel with baillie John Campbell . . . and one Robert Campbell, a scrubb wryterr [a petty solicitor]'. Ominously, however, Atholl was also told how: 'It would gall any body to see the insolent haughty carriage of our squade Lords, who meett and caball among themselves as if they were constitute governors by the sovereigne.'[25] Montrose, Roxburghe and Argyll were named in a long list of regents to form an interim administration until George's arrival in England. George's absolute trust in Argyll's support for the Hanoverian succession was signified more by the naming of the Duke as one of the triumvirate, with James Stanhope and Cadogan, which had been secretly appointed to make contingency planning for the armed defence of the succession if necessary, during Marlborough's absence at that time on the Continent.[26]

However, when Scottish offices were handed out, Montrose got the key Scottish political appointment, replacing Mar as third British secretary of state. Roxburghe got a sinecure as keeper of the Great Seal. Argyll, whose ambitions regarding the secretary's post would have been for his brother not himself, became groom of the stole to the Prince of Wales; while Ilay added the sinecure of lord clerk register to the office he had previously been granted for life, that of lord justice general. George I, at the time of his accession, hoped to have a government of king's friends without faction or party extremes. Tentative steps at the outset of his reign to recognise the loyalty of those who could be classed as Hanoverian Tories soon gave way, however, to a purge of Tories. The Peace of Utrecht concluded by the Tories was a source of anger. Greater concessions could have been wrung from France and Hanover's interests were betrayed.

That the squadrone got the better part of the spoils which fell to the Scottish Whigs may be accounted for by the influence, albeit waning, of the Junto. The first ministry of the reign was headed by Lord Halifax of the Junto (who died in May 1715). The problem of keeping august Argyll happy also remained. Nevertheless, Montrose started out as secretary of state at a time in which there was supposed to be a spirit of co-operation among the Scottish Whigs. In this atmosphere there was a weak attempt at an innovation to improve the government of

Scotland in the absence of the Privy Council, harking back to an ear-lier ill-fated idea of Harley's time, to have a 'commission of chamberlainry and trade'. The new attempt at innovation was the set-ting up at the end of 1714 of the commission of police. The idea had been suggested to Montrose in August by the Earl of Buchan, a politi-cal lightweight, 'as something in form of a Privy Council or Committee of Council for Scotland'. The squadrone interest seems to have slight-ly outweighed that of Argyll among the first members appointed, in that Buchan, an apparent neutral but who was spoken of as a political friend by one of the squadrone leaders, Rothes, was a member of the commission, as was Buchan's brother, and this tipped the scales. Most of the members were peers.

Duncan Forbes summarised their business as being: 'to present Min-isters to such Kirks as the King is Patron of; to notice nonjurors, papists, Highland Clans, the poor of the nation, Highways, Ports and Navigable Rivers &c.' – in other words, a mixture of suppression and improvements. The remit to make rivers navigable was added by Ilay on his own initiative before he passed the proposals on to the King's secretary. Tweeddale, the president of the commission, was to have a salary of £1200, the other peers £800 and the commoners £400, hand-some sums. Tweeddale suggested that they should meet at Holyrood House in the great apartment the commissioners to parliament had made use of.[27] The commission of police, which was suppressed in 1782, had no power, it did very little and, at a time when public initi-atives were always linked to political jobs, it quickly became just a useful source of patronage for lesser peers.

In this respect, it is surely no coincidence that the commission came into being at the height of the campaign to elect the first parliament of the new reign. This was an election in which the Whigs mounted a very determined and successful assault on the Tories, using patron-age and other means to get rid of them. The Tories had also lost popularity because of the threat the last administration of Anne's reign had posed to the Protestant succession. In Scotland 38 of the 45 mem-bers elected to the Commons were Whigs. The squadrone and Argyll had been instructed to co-operate during the election campaign, but the peace between them was not even surface deep. The squadrone were almost transfixed in their dread of Ilay, who gave them no rest. In particular, they found it difficult to counteract a wave of propa-ganda. A desperate Lord Rothes of the squadrone, who was trying to manage their affairs in Fife, spoke of a campaign of 'whispered things, that doe much harm'. He pleaded for help from Montrose, as it was 'absolutely necessary to stop this torrent'.

Ilay was said to be behind an address against the union – a popular cause – but this could not be proven. Rothes said that Colonel John Middleton (Ilay's closest political friend) 'and others who depend intirely on the brothers give it out pretty oppenly that both of 'em are for having the Union broke'. But, there again, John Campbell of Skipness, their candidate for Edinburgh, gave Rothes assurances to the contrary. The effect of the rumour was that the squadrone suffered the odium of being against the popular cause.[28] At this time, however, Ilay had much more work to do in building up the Argyll electoral interest and his hands were tied a bit by the enforced pact. For example, John Campbell ('Skip') failed to win Edinburgh, despite inducements to the Council; and Argyll, in an uneasy agreement with Montrose, accepted the re-election of the squadrone's friend, Thomas Smith, in the Glasgow burghs rather than pushing the claims of his preferred candidate, Daniel Campbell of Shawfield (Skip's brother). Argyll's friends had to wait until the next general election to gain these seats.

The first major casualty of the sharing of patronage between the squadrone and Argyll was Montrose, the secretary of state. The circumstances suggest that he was a secretary whose influence did not amount to much. With rebellion threatening, lord lieutenants were appointed in Scotland. Argyll, who as commander-in-chief in Scotland was a key figure in the suppression of insurrection, got the appointment in Dunbartonshire in preference to Montrose. He was also made lord lieutenant of Argyll and – a truer reflection of his status in the defence of the realm at the outset of the emergency – of Surrey. In August 1715 Montrose resigned as secretary. His allies in the squadrone were utterly dismayed. His relative, the Countess of Haddington, told him plainly that: 'by men that pushes ther fortoun it wil be thoght want of resolution and weakness in not being able to bear a disapointment'.[29]

Earlier in August Montrose's predecessor as secretary, Mar – whose career in mainstream politics had ended with George I's accession – embarked for Scotland, where he arranged a rendezvous at Braemar with the leaders of the disaffected Scottish nobility and gentry. He raised the Pretender's standard there in September. Argyll set out for Scotland to take command of the forces there and was shortly followed by Ilay. In due course Ilay proceeded to the town of Inveraray, the Duke's seat, to take command of the loyal people thereabouts. In an important incident, Mar ordered 'the clans' under General Gordon to march into Argyllshire and disarm this loyal following. They reached Invera-ray, but Ilay and his confederates contrived to delay them with protracted negotiations outside the town, and after several days the attempt upon the west Highlands was abandoned and the clans rejoined the main Jacobite force. On 13 November 1715, Mar and Argyll fought their inconclusive engagement at Sheriffmuir. The end result was in Argyll's favour since, as it has been said: 'it condemned Mar to weeks of further inactivity, and to the inevitable wastage of men which inactivity entailed upon a Highland army.'[30]

Argyll's leadership after Sheriffmuir in not pursuing and hunting down the rebels is commonly dismissed by historians as weak or dilatory, accepting the line pushed by his enemies in the Marlborough camp. It is easy to forget the political imperatives in Scotland that Argyll had to respond to. With the onset of a severe winter, the men in the Jacobite force would disperse and return to their homes. This they did, effectively ending the rebellion in Scotland. To embark upon a harsh campaign of attrition against them and to support punitive measures afterwards would have discredited Argyll, especially in Highland society. In other words, it would have wrecked his power base in Scotland which was being painstakingly consolidated by Ilay. This did not mean that Argyll was a Jacobite sympathiser. His closest henchman in Scotland, Duncan Forbes, understood this well. In an anonymous letter to Walpole, who had become first lord of the treasury in October 1715, Forbes later explained that to deal with the rebels with the utmost rigour and severity was to attack the whole Scottish nation, including the loyal people:

> I may venture to say, there are not 200 gentlemen in the whole kingdom who are not very nearly related to some one or other of the rebels. Is it possible that a man can see his daughter, his grandchildren, his nephews, or cousins, reduced to beggary and starving unnecessarily by a government, without thinking ill of it . . ..

Forbes himself believed the wisest course to be to punish as many 'as was necessary for terror', and then to be clement.[31]

After Sheriffmuir extra troops were sent to support Argyll. These included a detachment of 6000 Dutch troops under Cadogan, who had been at The Hague on diplomatic service. Cadogan complained about the dilatory measures of his commander, Argyll. After vigorous representations from Marlborough, Argyll was replaced as commander-in-chief in Scotland by Cadogan, Marlborough's crony, whose own relative inadequacy in doing the mopping up was attacked by Forbes. In summer 1716 when the emergency was over, Cadogan, who also had rewards awaiting for diplomatic services, was invested with the Order of the Thistle by the King and received a peerage. Argyll, and Ilay (who had been wounded at Sheriffmuir) were removed from all their offices, apart from Ilay's life appointment as justice general.

Unhappiness with the treatment meted out to rebels, including forfeiture, was the general context of Forbes's letter. The treatment meted out to Argyll was the specific context. Argyll's position was all the more vexing in that his military ambitions in his competition with Cadogan had been thwarted. Cadogan was to become, in effect, the head of the army in place of the failing Marlborough. Things had reached such a fever pitch that Argyll sent a gentleman to Cadogan to demand satisfaction for a small affront. Cadogan begged his pardon. Forbes chose, however, to misunderstand the reason for the Duke's dismissal. That was not so much through the lack of zeal shown by Argyll during the rebellion – although he lost clout with the ministry in consequence – as fear of the influence he might exercise upon the Prince of Wales during a long visit George I was about to make to Hanover.

Tensions were rising between the father and son at this time. Argyll was the Prince's groom of the stole. Walpole and his brother-in-law Townshend, secretary for the northern department, who were to remain in England when the King was in Hanover, were afraid that Argyll would take the chance to intrigue with the Prince against them. Argyll therefore had to be dismissed. Within a few weeks, however, he and Ilay, who had again reached that stage where they had little to lose, were constantly at Hampton Court with the Prince (the future George II). The alarmed Walpole kept the other secretary of state, Stanhope, who was in Hanover, in the picture about this. Walpole believed Argyll to be endeavouring to engage Tories and, particularly, 'whigs that he apprehends are disgusted'. This was to build up an independent parliamentary interest for the Prince.[32]

Argyll was 'constantly in parties of pleasure with the prince': 'they have begun little private balls . . .. The company are his highnesse, his grace's servants, the women, the maids of honour, and some of the dressers, and no spectators admitted.' The effect of this was all the more damaging in that Walpole and Townshend were dragged into the fray. Sunderland, who was now coming into the King's favour, was looking for just such an opening to attack Walpole and Townshend. It was Sunderland's ambition to supplant them with the Duke of Marlborough's friends.[33] He denounced Walpole and Townshend to the King as being in cahoots with Argyll and Ilay in plotting with the Prince. Walpole wrote to Stanhope that whoever had given this account of intrigues with 'the two brothers' would be found to be 'confounded liars'. Townshend later said that it was hard to conceive 'how so much villany and infatuation could possess the heart of any man as to suggest such an infamous accusation'.[34] He said this after being removed from his secretaryship in December, when he accepted the post of lord lieutenant of Ireland. When Townshend also lost this post in April 1717, Walpole resigned as first lord of the treasury.

Personal issues were not at the heart of the matter, however. The real problem was that Townshend's policy aims in northern Europe were at odds with those of the King and the other secretary, Stanhope. George, as elector of Hanover and King, was carefully working with Stanhope towards a peace plan for the north. Townshend had an agenda that interfered with this. There was also a view held by some of the Whigs, including Walpole, that Hanoverian priorities were dominating foreign affairs. Nevertheless, the personal divisions were critical in the major Whig schism at this time. On the one hand, there was the new group in power, led by Stanhope, Sunderland and Cadogan, 'the Marlborough faction'. On the other, there were the dissident Whigs, led by Walpole and Townshend and backed by the Prince of Wales. In the short term, the Scottish beneficiaries of the schism were the squadrone. There had been some dragging of feet, apparently by both the King and Walpole, in appointing Roxburghe successor to Montrose as third secretary. With the shift in power, Roxburghe got the post in December 1716. He and the squadrone benefited from their old attachment to Sunderland in the latter's former Junto guise and from other associations with the Marlborough faction. Duncan Forbes, in his anonymous letter to Walpole, railed against the squadrone and Cadogan for each in their own way blackening the reputation of Argyll as the King's general during the '15.

In the longer term, however, the Scottish beneficiaries of the division among the Whigs were Argyll and Ilay. There had been contacts between Walpole and Argyll in the period before the latter's dismissal; and it is curious that in the problems between them in 1716 lay the germs of reconciliation. Sunderland, in denouncing Walpole and Townshend before they were driven into opposition, had ensured the animosity of the brothers-in-law towards the old Marlborough clique, animosity just as felt by Argyll and Ilay. The logic of an attachment between Walpole and Argyll was inescapable, both in this and in the benefits of combining their strength in the House of Commons. Just one of the signs of this was the narrow escape of Cadogan in June 1717, when Walpole supported charges of corruption brought against the latter in the Commons. Cadogan was charged with embezzling funds provided for transporting the Dutch troops he commanded in the '15. He survived by ten votes. Among those who voted against him were 11 followers of Argyll.[35]

In 1719–20 there were signs that the King was seeking a reconciliation with the dissident Whigs. Ragnhild Hatton, in her analysis of the background to the outbreak of peace between the Whig factions at this time, concludes that the fact that in early 1720 the power of the two factions, those in and out of power, was about equal helped promote the reconciliation of the courts of the King and the Prince, which both the father and son by then desired.[36] She also makes the point that there were indications of the break-up of the Stanhope, Sunderland, Cadogan triumvirate. One of the first signs of change was the return to favour of Argyll in early 1719, although on modest terms and on the understanding that he did not have a say in Scottish affairs. Montrose's suspicion was that Argyll's return was engineered by Stanhope as a slight to Cadogan, as 'nobody doubts but that Lord Stan: don't love him'. Certainly Stanhope told Lord Stair, ambassador in Paris, in March 1719 that:

There has been since the two brothers came among us a good deal of jealousie and distrust among our friends. My good Lord Cadogan tho' he has made the utmost professions of friendship and deference to other folks' measures has certainly blown the coals. He has a notion of being premiere Ministre which I believe you will with me think a very Irish one, but however for the last two weeks bustled about extreamly among us and having been suffered under pretence of extraordinary zeal and diligence to recommend to several things out of his province. This has procured him a certain sett of followers among whom the discontent and grumbling of late has been most evident.[37]

Argyll's earldom of Greenwich, received from Queen Anne, was upped to a dukedom at this time, an honour with some symbolism, Greenwich being the place of George I's arrival in England. In April 1720 Walpole and Townshend returned to the administration, initially in second-rank posts.

The scene was now set for the fall of Roxburghe and the squadrone. Their downfall was contributed to by a measure they had supported, the Septennial Act of 1716, which allowed parliaments to continue for seven years instead of the previous three. The intention of the Act had been to curb the Tory opposition by creating a more stable and less costly regime in which to manage patronage, that is without the too-frequent hysteria of elections. Now it served Ilay as he continued carefully to restore and increase the strength of his brother's interest in Scotland. This was with the good wishes of Walpole, who became head of the ministry again in 1721, following the death of Stanhope and the resignation, during the South Sea crisis, of Sunderland. After the general election of 1722, George Baillie, erstwhile associate of Secretary Roxburghe, observed that: 'Argile, by the favour of the ministry, in the controverted elections for Scotland, has at least two-thirds of the Scots members in the House of Commons, and for what I know R has none who depend on him except the Advocat and one or two more.'[38] Roxburghe's indolence was matched by Ilay's industry.

The trouble with Roxburghe was that although he was a very determined character, much more so than Montrose, his determination was channelled in the wrong direction. There was no sign of effort in building up the squadrone's rather puny interest in Scotland. He managed to cling on as secretary until 1725 and even managed to continue receiving patronage for some clients. After Sunderland's death, Cadogan and Roxburghe had joined a new star in the political firmament, the ambitious Lord Carteret, in attempting to oust Walpole. In this way the dynastic opposition to Walpole and Argyll, which originated in the old Marlborough group was continued into a new generation. Carteret, secretary of state from 1721 to 1724, was a brilliant diplomatist who advanced George's foreign policy. Alliance with Carteret therefore gave Roxburghe the King's protection. George Baillie also surmised that Roxburghe might dexterously be using, 'the little jarrings of great men . . . by applying to each of them as he finds will answer his purpose'.[39] When Carteret was ousted in 1724, Roxburghe was finished. His last act was to condone, even encourage unrest and civil disobedience in Scotland in 1725 when the malt tax was applied there. This merely provided a fine triumph for Ilay, who at the behest of Walpole went north to Edinburgh and with a combination of diplomacy and the banging together of heads restored tranquillity, to Walpole's great satisfaction. Roxburghe was dismissed from office. Cadogan also went in 1725, when his post of master general of the ordnance was given to Argyll. Ilay became the political manager of Scotland on behalf of Walpole and the Argyll interest. A period of political stability began.

4

FROM ILAY TO DUNDAS

Archibald, Earl of Ilay, Third Duke of Argyll

Most of the Scots who attended parliament only hired houses or rooms in London. The practice was general among politicians from the whole of Great Britain so that the price of accommodation fell sharply when parliament rose. Scots would then return to Scotland or, if they had the means, to country houses in England. Most of the Scots were of modest means in comparison with the English members. Such generalisations hide the fact that the more important Scottish politicians, including Montrose, Roxburghe, Argyll and Ilay, were comfortable in London society and were sophisticated, well-travelled men. It may also be said that the integration of the Scottish landed elite into English society was well under way by mid century. Hazel Horn, in describing the lives of the Scots in London, observes that of the 16 representative peers in 1747 to 1752, seven had English wives (three of them having had two).[1] To this total we may add Ilay, whose estranged English wife died in 1723.

Another useful generalisation is that the Scots in parliament were usually a quiescent group, thanks to their dependence on ministerial patronage. The particular context in which this happened between 1722 and 1760, however, is equally relevant. This was the era of the monopolists, Argyll and his brother Ilay (who succeeded to the dukedom in 1743). Their absolute determination to dominate the political scene, in part through supporting the election of most of the parliamentary candidates, helped shape the general dependability of the Scottish representation; just as it was Argyll's own rebellious tendency which undermined that dependability in 1741. They were the 'two brothers to whom the whole country was realised'.[2] In view of the influence – dating back to the union – of the brothers in Scottish politics, their private lives, particularly Ilay's, merit scrutiny. A good look at their backgrounds also helps to humanise them in the face of the attribution that is commonly given to them as worthless 'magnates' (almost automatons), whose personality is defined by their class. There must be redeeming features.

The intensity of their lives outside Scotland affected the care they could give to Scotland beyond the narrow politics. The degree of attention they could devote to their own Scottish estates probably matches what they could do in promoting social and economic progress in Scotland as a whole, had they so wished and had their power to do so not been limited. In the management of the Argyll estates, there was some sign of neglect by the soldier Duke, although this, in the later years, must have been partly because he did not have a son and heir. When Ilay succeeded as Duke the estates were given much more attention. He did this with great help from Lord Milton. The latter was a lawyer who took the courtesy title of 'Lord Milton' as a judge. His real name was Andrew Fletcher and he owned the lands of Saltoun in East Lothian. He was nephew of the famous patriot. The new Duke and Milton visited Inveraray every year in the late summer and autumn (apart from 1745 when their stay was cut short) and corresponded about the management at other times. The Duke embarked on the building of Inveraray Castle even though he did not have a legitimate son to inherit it. His successor was his cousin, 'the very handsome, very stupid' old soldier, Jack Campbell.

Before becoming Duke, Ilay was very interested in the small estate he had bought outside Edinburgh, the Whim, relying on Milton to carry out his wishes in an elaborate drainage scheme. He also made occasional political visits to Scotland. And he sometimes exercised his right as lord justice general to preside, to some purpose, over the supreme criminal court, the court of justiciary, where the lord justice clerk normally presided, Milton holding that office from 1735 to 1748. When in England, however, Ilay was engaged in private enthusiasms that bore no relevance to Scotland. Outside the narrow range of parliamentary affairs, and the political management he conducted with the help of the ministry in London and by correspondence with Milton in Edinburgh, these enthusiasms generally absorbed him. Apart from politics and during exceptional periods as in the aftermath of the Jacobite rising of 1745, (the '45), Ilay's one abiding interest in Scottish business was in the House of Lords. He dominated proceedings in appeals heard there from the head civil court in Scotland, the court of session; and even these could have a political dimension. The lives of the second Duke and Ilay in the south also help to reveal their personalities and the elements in their background that affected their political behaviour and reduced their influence. One end-product of such factors was Argyll's defection to the opposition. Another was Ilay's failure to become a top-rank politician. They were both born at Ham House, at Petersham, beside the Thames west of London. Ham House was the home of their maternal grandmother, the Countess of Dysart and her second husband, the Duke of Lauderdale. Her first husband, Argyll and Ilay's grandfather, was Sir Lionel Tollemache, a Suffolk landowner. Lauderdale, one of Charles II's committee of ministers, the cabal, monopolised Scottish business at court for about ten years from 1667. He died in 1682, the year in which Ilay was born and when Argyll was about four. The Countess died at Ham House in 1698. She was a singular personality. Perhaps we should resist seeking parallels with the characters of one or other of her Campbell grandsons – her ambition and ruthless determination to achieve her ends, her study of mathematics and philosophy, her say (as Lauderdale's Duchess) in the control of patronage.

Argyll's military career from a young age on the Continent has already been mentioned. Ilay was educated at Eton. At the age of 17 he went to Glasgow University and then studied law at Utrecht. His education, as a younger son without estates, was designed to make him a man of business and it strengthened his associations with Scotland. He also had brief military experience. Undoubtedly, he spent much of his youth in England, west of London. I have previously followed *The Scots Peerage* in saying that he lived in England until going to Glasgow. But he and his brother will also have spent spells at the homes of their mother, Elizabeth Tollemache, at Duddingston near Edinburgh and in Kintyre, where she farmed. They also became playmates of George Lockhart in their infancy.[3] The Duchess was separated for years from their father, the first Duke (died 1703). Also to be taken into account is that the family estates in Argyll, which had been forfeited, were not restored to their father until the revolution.

The brothers loved Petersham. Argyll built Sudbrook House there in bucolic seclusion beside Richmond Park. He lived at Sudbrook with his second Duchess and their five daughters, 'the screaming Campbells'.

Ilay was more than content with simpler surroundings across the Thames, at Whitton, near Twickenham in Middlesex. He carved a small estate there out of the wilderness of Hounslow Heath. These homes had the inestimable advantage of being near one of the royal palaces, Hampton Court, and other royal houses. Argyll also built a house at Adderbury in Oxfordshire. And he and Ilay had property and houses in London, in the Great Marlborough Street area. In 1736 the development of Argyll Street began on the Duke's estate there. For a short time Argyll also owned Kenwood House, beside Hampstead Heath. In 1715 he conveyed it to Ilay and their brother-in-law the second Earl of Bute (died 1723).[4] These lords did not occupy it personally.

Ilay, said Horace Walpole, 'had a great thirst for books; a head admirably turned to mechanics; was a patron of ingenious men, a promoter of discoveries, and one of the first great encouragers of planting in England.' When Sir John Clerk called at Ilay's house in Great Marlborough Street in 1733, he saw a very large room in which he kept his library, containing a vast collection of books and all sorts of curiosities, particularly mathematical instruments, all lying 'in a very careless phylosophic manner'.[5] When Ilay built a new library in 1743 it was 90 feet long, 27 feet broad and 21 feet high, with galleries at either end: he considered it one of the finest rooms in London and it gave him 'great joy'.[6] Among hints of Ilay's position in London society, a position which naturally improved after he became Duke, were his role in the 1750s as one of the most active of the early trustees of the British Museum; and the credit he is given by Lady Mary Wortley Montagu for having made the collection of antique china fashionable.[7] His big achievement was as the 'treemonger', as Horace Walpole called him, who enriched the Thames landscape with the introduction of foreign trees and plants. Walpole said that he 'contributed essentially to the richness of colouring so peculiar to our modern landscape'.[8]

Despite all this, he was always a bit of an outsider in ruling circles. In part the problem seems to have been that he was not quite of the right background. Among the many insults hurled at him and his brother, accusations of Scottishness are hard to find and assessments of their oratory do not refer to their accents. But if we take Ilay's education, there is an exotic quality. Most of the people in English ministerial circles in the eighteenth century went first to Eton (which helps explain later vendettas) or Westminster School and then to colleges in Cambridge or Oxford. Glasgow College after Eton was a distinct oddity, setting Ilay apart. Nor was the way in which he pursued his obsessions quite right. Lady Louisa Stuart somehow hit the nail on the head when she said that: 'his humble companions were the ingenious and men who assisted him in his scientific pursuits, or those whose inventions he patronised.'[9] Ilay was not quite the landed gentleman.

In November 1733, on his way to Houghton, the Norfolk seat of Walpole, who was a great huntsman, Ilay wrote to Milton that: 'As I don't hunt, I shall have time enough at Houghton to write about every thing.' A letter about political payments to indigent Scots peers followed from Houghton: 'Ld Rea is come right and may have the £100 when he will. Cromarty must also have another 100, and Lord Rollo also 100. You may give Cromarties [sic] to Lord Elibank. Remit Rea's by whom you please, and for Rollo's he has a son in Edinburg a goldsmith, or any other way you find best.'[10]

Argyll and Ilay were a tribulation to each other. The worst aspect was the distress in the Argyll household at the looming prospect of Ilay's succession to the dukedom. Matters reached such a pitch that there were long periods in which the brothers used intermediaries to communicate. William Steuart MP acted as a messenger between them for many years. Lord Hervey reported that: 'by the means of a Mr Stuart, who went between them, an adroit fellow and a common friend to them both, they acted as much in concert as if they both had been the most intimate and most cordial friends.'[11] Ilay's political life was damaged badly by the stormy character of Argyll. After the latter's death Ilay remarked to Milton that: 'The great error in my brother's conduct was that he was too apt to quarrel and knew whom he fought against, but never considered whom he fought for.'[12]

Damage was also inflicted on both of them by their friendship with Mrs Henrietta Howard, later Countess of Suffolk, the former mistress of the Prince of Wales (George II). For years Ilay was a good friend to Mrs Howard. He acted for her in the early 1720s in the purchase of the small Marble Hill estate, where she built her house next door to the riverside home in Twickenham (now Orleans House) of the old Scottish secretary, James Johnston. She remained friendly with the future king. A contemporary, Lord Hervey, came to the uncharitable conclusion that the brothers were among those who cultivated her friendship merely to strengthen their position at court. Mrs Howard certainly believed that after the Prince of Wales became King in 1727, they consciously abandoned her. By then they had found that the real power at court was Queen Caroline. Whatever the nature of their friendship with Mrs Howard, they suffered because of it. The Queen, who died in 1737, restrained Ilay from prospering as he might. She tolerated him only because of his importance to her great friend Walpole in support of the ministry. Hervey paraphrased words spoken by Lord Stair during an audience with Caroline in which Stair foolishly denounced Walpole:

> The only two men in this country who ever dared to attempt to set a mistress's power up in opposition to yours were Lord Ilay and his brother the Duke of Argyll; yet one of the men who strove to dislodge you by this method from the King's bosom is the man your favourite has thought fit to place nearest to his.[13]

This, and George II's coolness towards Argyll and Ilay, dating from 1719 when the brothers were the first to relinquish George's cause in his squabble with his father, help explain why Ilay never received the post of secretary of state. English reluctance to increase the power of the house of Argyll in Scotland also affected matters. Ilay had to be content with the role of political manager of Scotland on behalf of several ministries, while holding the sinecure of keeper of the Privy Seal of Scotland. His influence in shaping Scottish affairs outside the realm of narrow politics was, in short, restrained.

When Ilay became Walpole's Scottish political manager in 1725 – a role he had effectively held since before the election of 1722, though less formally – Walpole controlled the treasury and was master of the House of Commons. Walpole managed the Commons by his very effective performance in debate, by keeping the land tax low, by pursuing a pacific foreign policy, and by using patronage to give him a 'reliable phalanx' of court supporters.[14] For most of the Walpole period, Ilay managed Scotland with support in matters of government patronage from Walpole at the treasury, and with less enthusiastic help from the Duke of Newcastle, secretary of state. With the concurrence and support of Argyll, who was not close to Walpole, Ilay made a handsome contribution to Walpole's dominance of the Commons, presenting him with a large block of loyal Scottish MPs. He also assisted in securing a generally compliant group of representative peers to sit in the Lords. These Scots sat squarely at the centre of British politics in their adherence to Walpole.

However, the few Scots who were in opposition to Ilay and Walpole were no less part of the British political mainstream in the 'country' politics they followed. In September 1725 Walpole stressed to the then secretary for the northern department, Townshend, that Ilay had agreed not to 'aim to ingross the whole power of Scotland into his own hands'. A token of this agreement was the small share of patronage that the much-weakened squadrone and other opponents of Ilay continued to receive in the years following. For example, Montrose kept his post as keeper of the Great Seal. The receipt of at best modest patronage, however, was poor compensation for being excluded from political power. The squadrone and other thwarted elements in Scotland, led by Lord Stair, who was a former Marlborough adherent and looked upon Ilay as an upstart, joined therefore with the opposition to Walpole in England. This opposition, both Whig and Tory, combined under the country banner. They also called themselves 'the patriots'. They claimed to defend the interests and liberties of the country as a whole against the ministry of Walpole, 'the GRAND CORRUPTOR'. Lord Bolingbroke used this phrase. He, with William Pulteney, another frustrated politician of great ability, founded *The Craftsman*, a weekly periodical that intellectualised the voice of opposition. Bolingbroke's brilliant writing gave it great appeal and it attacked Walpole to effect. Bolingbroke, it should be mentioned, had fled to France in 1715, where he actively supported the Jacobites. Walpole had led the way in hounding him. And although Bolingbroke was allowed to return home in 1723, he was stopped by Walpole from sitting in the House of Lords.

The opposition mounted an attack on Walpole in 1733. The occasion was a bill he brought in to introduce excise duties on tobacco and wine (in place of lesser customs duties). This would enable the land tax to be reduced. The fiscal change should have had some attraction for country gentlemen, but there had been an effective campaign against it. In the face of a collapsing majority in the Commons and of popular clamour, Walpole ultimately abandoned the measure. Shortly thereafter, the ministry almost lost a vote in the Lords on a matter unrelated to the excise bill. Montrose, Stair and others who voted against Walpole were summarily dismissed from their posts.

Walpole and Ilay's control of the Scottish parliamentary vote was damaged much more severely by an incident that, at first sight, seemed to have nothing to do with the opposition attacks upon them. In 1736 the court of justiciary condemned to death John Porteous, captain of the Edinburgh town guard. He had been put on trial after ordering his men to fire on a disorderly crowd at the public execution of a smuggler, an incident in which six people were killed. A stay of execution of his sentence was granted by Queen Caroline, acting as regent. A mob thereupon took the law into their own hands, broke into the jail and lynched Porteous on a dyer's post near the spot where the people had been killed. Amidst outrage in London a bill was brought in containing punitive measures against the city of Edinburgh and threatening its privileges. Walpole countenanced the bill; Ilay, involved as so often in damage limitation, accepted it reluctantly; Argyll and Scotland as a whole bitterly opposed it.[15] A much watered-down version of the bill finally received the royal assent, but the harm was done. From this point, Argyll's disenchantment with Walpole really began. He did not declare this openly, however, until 1739. He then joined the opposition who, in the face of Walpole's reluctance, were pushing for war with Spain in a dispute about British trading rights in Spain's Caribbean possessions (the War of Jenkins's Ear).

The political consequences of the Porteous affair for Walpole and Scotland were not just the chance outcome of spontaneous English outrage and anti-Scottish prejudice. The attack on Edinburgh in parliament arose out of an enquiry, humiliating to Scotland, in the House of Lords into the particulars of the affair. Walpole's old enemy Carteret, who had narrow political motives in mind, proposed the enquiry. Lord Hervey, a close associate of Walpole's, had no doubt that 'Carteret's reason for stirring this inquiry' was to make the administration incur Scottish resentment by reacting harshly, or face criticism in England for being too lenient. Carteret also wished to show the Scots that: 'by taking the Campbells to govern them, they had chosen governors that could not protect them.' Hervey observed that Walpole did not want the enquiry, partly because he did not want to make a national issue of the affair and also because: 'he feared it might hurt Lord Ilay, for he had no more mind to be thought incapable of protecting Lord Ilay than Lord Ilay had a mind to be thought incapable of protecting the Scotch.'[16]

At the general election of 1741, Walpole and Ilay were damaged by Argyll's defection. It was impossible for Ilay to manage the election effectively when the Argyll interest was split, even though he used ministerial patronage to assist in the campaign. Richard Scott, in his analysis of the election, dismisses accusations that Ilay secretly supported his brother against Walpole. In some constituencies, including Ayrshire and the Aberdeen burghs, pro-Argyll opposition candidates and pro-Ilay government candidates actually clashed. While Ilay and

Milton did what they could to secure the return of as many Walpole adherents as possible, Argyll actively supported the opposition in several constituencies.[17] As a result, only 19 of the Commons' seats in Scotland – perhaps nine of them pro-Ilay and the remainder independent Whigs – were held by Walpole, compared with 30 before the election. The interest of Frederick, Prince of Wales, who had his own faction in opposition, took seven of the ten seats that Walpole also lost in Cornwall. It may be added that Argyll had the additional support in England of George Bubb Dodington and the latter's small group of MPs. By the end of the year Walpole's majority could be counted at only 16, in large part because of the losses in Scotland and Cornwall.[18] His position was further weakened by lack of success in the war with Spain and by the King's declaration of Hanover's neutrality in the conflict that had broken out in Europe over the Austrian succession. Walpole, no longer in control of the Commons, retired from the fray in February 1742. Argyll died in October 1743. Historians, in studying the ebb and flow of politics, often underestimate the ravages of age. Instead of stressing John, Duke of Argyll's motives in his last years, we might consider his health. His prickly temper finally gave way to depression and paranoia. It was not surprising that he went into opposition again soon after a new administration was formed in 1742.

The new ministry embraced both 'old corps' Whigs from the Walpole administration and the 'new Whigs' representing the former opposition, namely the so-called 'patriots' consisting of the Prince of Wales's faction and those who had followed Pulteney and Carteret. Carteret dominated the ministry. The main Scottish political beneficiary, that is apart from senior posts in the army received by the failing Duke of Argyll, briefly, and then Lord Stair, was the fourth Marquis of Tweeddale. He represented himself, but may be looked upon as a remnant of the squadrone. His friend Carteret revived the post of third secretary of state for him. Ilay, Duke of Argyll from 1743, accepted this with a good grace, almost with some complacency. He calmed Milton, his lieutenant in Edinburgh: 'I had your letters by which I perceive you have been in the vapours, and in answer to them I can only say, *tranqualisez vous*.'[19] This sanguine approach was justified. Carteret did not want a divisive regime in Scotland and the new Duke of Argyll was then on good terms with him, which helped Argyll in preserving the offices of his adherents. Tweeddale also lacked political talent.

Milton, meanwhile, as lord justice clerk reporting from Scotland loyally and dutifully to Tweeddale on public affairs – on the uppishness of the Jacobites in particular – quickly regained his customary equilibrium. He lost authority in patronage matters at this time but, through sheer talent and determination, almost remained as he had been since the late 1720s, the political top dog in Scotland on behalf of his master, Duke Archibald in London. Milton, as ever, was adept in using his post as lord justice clerk to take on the role of senior public servant. His talent and industry were without parallel in Scotland. They were matched only by the chagrin of Robert Dundas, younger of Arniston, who was Tweeddale's solicitor-general, and of others whose hopes of political mastery were thwarted. Tweeddale's correspondent and political representative in Edinburgh, Thomas Hay of Huntington, a pleasant, moderate man, could not cope with the audacious Milton and with Tweeddale's failure of leadership.

Before and during the Jacobite rebellion, Milton befriended and advised the English generals, Cope and Guest. In February 1746, two months before Culloden, the Duke of Cumberland, who had taken command, wrote from Scotland to Newcastle: 'The Justice Clark is as able and willing a man as there exists, but too much an Argyle man to be trusted with all that will be necessary in this affair. This I say to you and you allone for he is of vast use to me and does all I want with the greatest readiness imaginable.'[20] In the aftermath of the rebellion Milton added to his already great political authority in Scotland. He corresponded with ministers, looked after intelligence operations, prepared evidence for trials, smoothed relations between the military and civil authorities, enforced the new laws against non-juring meeting houses, and organised the transportation of Jacobite prisoners to England.[21]

As for Tweeddale, he resigned in January 1746 from his post as third secretary of state, which then lapsed permanently. His protector, Carteret, had been forced out of office in 1744, in part for supporting the King's costly pro-Hanover policy. The old corps Whigs, led by Newcastle's brother, Henry Pelham, who became first lord of the treasury in 1743, gradually reasserted their supremacy and in 1746, the new Duke of Argyll resumed his role as political manager of Scotland.

He had a good relationship with Pelham (who died in 1754) and, at best, an uneasy working one with Newcastle, secretary of state. Pelham wished, even more than Walpole had done, to avoid placing too much power into Argyll's hands. He also wished to keep as many of the Scottish Whigs as he could loyal to the ministry. Argyll understood and accepted this. The proof was a rather more equitable sharing out of patronage than in Walpole's time. The prime example was the appointment in 1748 of Robert Dundas of Arniston, a squadrone man, as lord president of the court of session, a thing that would not have been tolerated under the Walpole-Ilay regime. However, referring to tensions within the ministry, Scott believes that the major English politicians' main interest in Scotland at this time was to use it to strengthen their own positions.[22] But the shallow politics did not go on quite as before. In the years after the rebellion, Argyll's most testing problem was an anti-Scottish backlash. The latter was not general, but was whipped up by Cumberland, who considered most Scots to be passive Jacobites. Newcastle and the English lord chancellor, Hardwicke, gave Cumberland their support if not their conviction; while Pelham, not wishing to alienate the Scots, supported Argyll in mitigating the effects. Of the legislation that followed, the Act abolishing heritable jurisdictions brought about the most beneficial structural change by reducing the powers of the Highland magnates to oppress their people. The Act with the most retrograde social consequences was the Disarming Act. This included a provision to ban Highland dress, which Milton correctly feared would cause hardship for poor innocent people. Jacobitism itself, however, was a spent force and English fear of insurrection in Scotland gradually declined as time passed. A new political era for Scotland was about to begin.

After Pelham's death Newcastle headed the ministry. For a time he worked zealously to establish a personal faction in Scotland. He attempted, without admitting it, to undermine Argyll's mastery of Scotland, as Alexander Murdoch explains. Among Newcastle's moves was the construction of quite an ambitious network of correspondents in opposition to Argyll and the advancement of placemen, including the appointment of Robert Dundas younger of Arniston as lord advocate. Newcastle's justification for interfering in Scottish affairs was that the existence of a Scottish viceroy was a barrier to complete union between Scotland and England.[23] It is equally valid to point to Newcastle's jealousy of his fellow secretaries of state in the 1740s and early 1750s as paralleling his attitude to Argyll. Newcastle himself was under threat. He could not provide the House of Commons with leadership; he frustrated the ambitions of Henry Fox and William Pitt; the ministry's pro-Hanover foreign policy was under attack; and relations between the British and the French in North

America and India were beyond crisis point. Fox and Argyll, both past associates under Walpole, joined forces to add to Newcastle's discomfiture. By summer 1755 Newcastle, whose Scottish support in the Commons fell for a time to only three members out of the 45, conceded the point and began to mend bridges in earnest. After courting Argyll in the autumn, he accepted the latter's demands in Scottish business in total.[24]

War with France was declared in May 1756. Newcastle was out of office from the following October until June 1757, when he formed a ministry with Pitt, a broad-bottom administration, that is one with cross-party appeal. The outbreak of the Seven Years' War smothered incipient divisions within the Whig ranks. And the war, a great and popular national cause, hastened remarkably the integration of the Scots into the British nation. The popularity in Scotland of Pitt, who managed the war effort, was evidence of change not just a symbol of it. His championship of the old Bolingbroke version of the country creed, with its special appeal to patriotism, went down well there. A curious feature was that Pitt was remote from Scottish affairs yet was popular in Scotland: the landed classes and middling orders in Scotland were becoming truly British. At the same time, the war undermined entrenched attitudes towards Scotland, even at the heart of the English political oligarchy. Scotland's vital contribution to the war effort included the raising of 26 regiments. Pitt later recalled that these, 'the very rebels', were thereby employed 'in the service and defence of their country': 'They were reclaimed by this means; they fought our battles; they cheerfully bled in defence of those liberties which they had attempted to overthrow but a few years before.'[25] Argyll himself, 'the old governor of Scotland' as Newcastle called him, got great credit for his part in helping to raise the troops. It was an Indian summer for him. In the few years before his death in 1761, his stock was far higher than it had ever been in his political career. Through his contribution to the war effort, he finally won over the King. The new force in Scottish affairs, however, was his nephew John Stuart, Earl of Bute.

Bute, Wilkes and Liberty

Bute was born in 1713. His mother was Anne Campbell, sister of the second and third Dukes of Argyll. When Bute's father died in 1723, these brothers were appointed guardians of Bute and his brother James Stuart Mackenzie (who took the name Mackenzie upon succeeding to an inheritance). Bute spent his infancy in Scotland, before going to Eton. His daughter, Lady Louisa Stuart, says that 'he returned no more to Scotland till almost a man; but passed his holidays at the home of one of his uncles', most frequently that of Duke John. At Sudbrook, Bute was one of the family. He later supported Duke John's defection from the Walpole administration. Upon being excluded from the list of representative peers in 1741 as a punishment for opposition, Bute retired to his seat at Mountstuart on the Isle of Bute. When rebellion broke out in Scotland in 1745 he returned to London.

A chance encounter with Frederick, Prince of Wales, led in due course to his appointment as lord of the bedchamber in the Prince's household. After Frederick's death in 1751, Bute remained a close and influential family friend of the dowager Princess of Wales, Augusta. In 1755 he was appointed finishing tutor to her son, George, Prince of Wales, the future George III, who developed a sort of hero-worship for him. Although the influence of Duke Archibald upon his nephew Bute can be discerned, for example in the enthusiasm for botany Bute inherited from that great plantsman, Bute evinced political independence. From the mid 1750s he had a small group of friends in Scotland who acted outside the Argyll interest. He actually quarrelled with Duke Archibald in electoral matters. This happened particularly in the Ayr burghs during the last couple of years of the Duke's life. Given the Duke's advanced age, a rivalry between the generations may have been a factor in the clash. In any case, these squabbles came at the tail end of the old regime. A new regime under George III had begun. The first great period of the political management of Scotland was over. Upon George's accession and following the brief rise to power of his favourite Bute, there was a long period of instability within the political elite. During these unstable times, Scotland's part in the political process was almost irrelevant. There was not even a role for Scots as before in contributing a body of loyal support to the ministry through the studied, long-term efforts of a political manager. However, the resentment towards Bute, which was displayed as an attack on his Scottishness, provides, in a most contrary way, a startling glimpse of the success of the Scots in taking advantage of the union, despite their inconsequentiality in parliamentary politics.

Bute had some interest in Scottish affairs. His political spats with Duke Archibald suggest this, as does his patronage of the Scottish universities

from 1760, described by Roger Emerson.[26] However, his sudden elevation to power under George III, becoming a secretary of state in 1761,
then first lord of the treasury in 1762, gave him much more pressing
business in London. He had also, not so very long before, been concerned in encouraging the patriotic principles of the young heir to the
throne, principles inimical to faction and corruption. The sort of Scottish business involving political management was therefore alien to Bute.
He handed this role over to his reluctant brother, who was much more
interested in continuing a diplomatic career. Bute justified the need
for political management as a means of protecting his uncle's old
friends. In Murdoch's assessment, the threat Bute was concerned with
was that of a more Anglocentric regime being introduced by Newcastle.[27] From 1761 to 1763 therefore, James Stuart Mackenzie in London
went into partnership with Milton in Edinburgh. Milton was still able
at this time, but lapsed into senile dementia in 1764. Unfortunately,
Mackenzie had neither the inclination nor the aptitude to knuckle down
to the work of management, though he dutifully and respectfully tried
to learn from Milton.

In any case, there was a dramatic change when Bute, who did not
have the stomach for the political fight, resigned from office in April
1763. He was unpopular, both as the King's favourite and as a Scotsman who had been forced upon the country. He had concluded a
peace treaty with France and Spain on unambitious, very unpopular
terms. His ministry had introduced a hated excise duty on cider; a
tax that was all the more contentious because the areas it affected did
not include Scotland. And the enemies who surrounded him included Pitt – a popular icon – as well as the Duke of Newcastle and his
group. These people had been forced out of office, in part because
they did not agree with Bute's foreign policy. Bute and George also
wished to end the Whig hegemony and the faction and corruption
they believed this represented – instead, they wanted to establish the
reign of the patriot king, as in the Bolingbroke model. Upon resign-
ing Bute tried, with the support of the King, to preserve Mackenzie's
role as Scottish manager and proposed to exclude the new head of the
ministry, George Grenville, from Scottish affairs. This improbable idea
mattered very little and did not come to much. Mackenzie lost his position in 1765. Fears at Westminster of Bute's influence 'behind the
curtain' persisted for years, but were largely unjustified; and his writ
no longer ran in Scotland.

Other leading Scottish politicians in the years that followed had varying levels of influence, by far the strongest of them being Sir Lawrence Dundas. But none attained the role of manager at a time of flux in which there was a succession of brief ministries. George III's attack upon party and faction had contributed to destabilising politics at the centre of government. His mistrust of a series of first ministers made matters worse. And this was at a time in which the party structure was already weak. The old issues differentiating the Whigs from the Tories had faded (so much so, indeed, that the attribution of these labels from then on, whether by contemporaries or historians, sometimes tends to confuse instead of elucidate). Not until composure returned to government was it possible, or even useful, to have a Scottish manager. Instead, a series of secretaries for the northern department gave desultory attention to Scottish business.

In the political polemic of the 1760s, however, Scotland was well to the fore. John Wilkes made sure of that. The imposition of Bute upon the nation was the catalyst of Wilkes's attack upon the Scots in general. The main vehicle of this assault was the weekly periodical, launched by Wilkes in June 1762, ironically titled *The North Briton*. In it he jocularly pretended to be a North Briton, a Scot, who was avoiding Scotticisms in his writing. It was a fashionable literary conceit in that period for the narrator to take on a role in this way. Wilkes set the tone early on: 'I own I cannot conceal the joy I feel as a North Briton; and I heartily congratulate my dear countrymen on our now at length accomplished the great, long sought, and universally national object of all our wishes, the planting a Scotsman at the head of the English Treasury.' Some of Wilkes's material displayed the pettiest of prejudice, but it can raise an innocent chuckle, as in the following mock news item, in which he made a valiant attempt at the Scots vernacular: 'Yesterday morning the two new-raised regiments of Highland guards were reviewed in Hyde Park by his grace the Duke of Inverness, who was pleased to say, "They kenn'd their business right weel, and went through their exercise very connily."' His work was a response to specific anxieties about the alien Scottish threat to the rights of the Englishman, rights associated with the Whig ideal of the liberties enjoyed by Saxon freemen. Wilkes reported in July 1762: 'Some time since died Mr John Bull, a very worthy, plain, honest, old gentleman, of Saxon descent; he was choaked by inadvertently swallowing a thistle, which he had placed by way of ornament on the top of his sallad. For many years before he had enjoyed a remarkably good state of health.'

Behind the call for the defence of English liberties, a very popular cause, there was the blunt fact that Scots were benefiting obtrusively from the union.[28] In these terms the union was, from an English point of view, proving to be just too successful for the Scots. This success was a challenge to the colonial attitudes still held by some in England. The attitude of the Duke of Newcastle was a case in point. During his spells as first lord of the treasury in the 1750s he worked comfortably with an Anglo-Scottish treasury expert, Lord Dupplin. Another Anglo-Scot, the attorney general William Murray, the member for Boroughbridge, was important to him in the House of Commons before becoming lord chief justice of the King's Bench and taking a peerage as Lord Mansfield in 1756. But Newcastle was accustomed to having the upper hand in dealing with Scots. It was no surprise therefore that his resentment against the influence of Bute was expressed in the words of a shocked Englishman whose world was turning upside down. The King, when opening the first parliamentary session of the new reign, declared that: 'Born and educated in this country, I glory in the name of Britain.' These ringing words, indicating George's zeal for Great Britain in preference to Hanover, were met with wide approval; but Newcastle and his friends did not like them. Newcastle thought the use of the term 'Britain' was remarkable. It denoted the Scottish author of the speech, Bute, to all the world. Newcastle (anticipating Wilkes) would have much preferred 'England'.[29]

Similar resentment towards Scots is found in the letters of 'Junius', which were published between 1767 and 1772 in the *Public Advertiser* and then copied by other newspapers. The favourite object of Junius's anger was the influence of Mansfield upon the law of England. As for the union, Junius believed it to be 'invariably directed by the advantage and interest of the Scots'. At the end of the century, it was not uncommon for people to allude to the 'empire' in Europe: this covered the three kingdoms controlled by England – England, Scotland and Ireland.[30] Colonial attitudes towards Scotland had, however, by then lost their force. The unnatural jolt caused by Bute's sudden elevation to power was no more than a memory and the integration of Scotland into the United Kingdom had continued.

The presence of the Scots was prominent in some fields of endeavour. By the mid 1760s about a fifth to a third of the officers in the army were Scots. They were also heavily represented in the army of the East India Company, in its civilian offices in Madras and Bengal and, thanks to patronage by Bute when secretary of state, in the new colonies of East and West Florida. Sixteen infantry regiments and three regiments of fencibles were raised in Scotland during the American War of Independence, for service not only in America, but also in India and as garrison forces in Ireland and Gibraltar.[31] The raising of regiments was undertaken by landlords, partly as a means of getting officers' posts for their sons. It should be added that the recruitment of soldiers for the regiments involved some coercion and misrepresentation about military life. This helps explain the mutinies of six Highland regiments between 1778 and 1783.[32] It is also an example of how the Scots had to work hard for their opportunities. Comfortable posts in the British home administration were not theirs for the taking. Thus the long development of the small Whitehall bureaucracy into a southern mandarin class at ease with itself seems not to have been greatly troubled by Scots interlopers during the eighteenth century. In politics, the greatest sign of acceptance of the Scots came in the final quarter of the century with the rise of Henry Dundas.

Henry Dundas, Viscount Melville

Henry Dundas has been the subject of traditional biographies and of more recent scholarly work, particularly that of Michael Fry and David Brown.[33] What follows therefore is simply a very brief outline of certain features of his career to summarise his place in the history of eighteenth-century Scotland. The tail end of Dundas's career after the resignation of Pitt in 1801 is not really part of the story. Dundas managed Scotland on behalf of Addington from April 1802 until June 1803, when his services were dispensed with. His Scottish allies contributed to the fall of the Addington administration in April 1804. He then joined the last Pitt administration and took on the Scottish management again.[34] He resigned from the government in April 1805, and faced unsuccessful impeachment proceedings in 1806 on a charge of malversion of public funds when he was treasurer of the navy.

Dundas was from a Midlothian landed family of modest means, the Dundases of Arniston, generations of whom had made successful careers in the law and public life. Their full potential had not been realised after the union because of their opposition to the Dukes of Argyll. Henry was born in 1742. He followed the family tradition in becoming an advocate. From 1766 to 1775 he held the relatively junior government post of solicitor-general for Scotland. In 1774 he entered parliament, as the member for Midlothian. His career in the

Commons lasted until 1802, latterly as the member for Edinburgh. He received a peerage at the end of 1802 and died in 1811. There is no purpose in attaching a party label to him. He was a career politician who was not concerned with party ideology, although some examples of an early reformist tinge can be pointed to. His closest colleague, William Pitt, described himself as an 'independent Whig', but Dundas could hardly be called that.

He held several offices, of which the following are the important ones from the present point of view. The first key appointment, in 1775, was that of lord advocate in the North administration, obtained partly with the help of Lord Mansfield. Dundas remained lord advocate until 1783. In 1781 he was appointed chairman of a committee of investigation into the war in the Carnatic. He became an expert in Indian affairs in consequence. He was a commissioner of the new board of control, 1784–93 and its president, 1793–1801, dominating in both capacities. He was home secretary, 1791–94. This post included responsibility for Scotland, in which he delegated much to his nephew, Robert Dundas of Arniston, lord advocate 1789–1801. Henry was single-minded in pursuit of his career. In this, Scotland was for him both a prize in itself and source of strength. In setting out his plans he was fortunate in forming an alliance, from about the end of late 1771, with the congenial young Duke of Buccleuch, who was based in Scotland. Their partnership lasted for 40 years. From the outset, they took an interest in election matters, in particular a number of struggles in the Lothians and elsewhere before the general election of 1774, using Buccleuch's influence and political interest so that when Dundas entered parliament after the election, a small group of friends joined him.[35]

Dundas soon made an impact in the Commons. In February 1778 he angered the King by speaking against Lord North's proposals to treat with the Americans. In November 1781, having changed his views, he created a great stir by speaking out against further attempts to recover America. But he had become, as David Brown puts it, the government's 'linchpin' in the Commons and was supportive of the faltering North government during the last stages of the war. He was a fine debater. His great asset, however, was his fearlessness, shown by his willingness, for example, to speak out on behalf of ministers, no matter the unpopularity of what he was saying. His electoral influence in Scotland was growing also. Yet North avoided handing him the managership of Scotland.

This was reflected in the uneasy relationship in patronage and electoral matters between Dundas and fellow Scot Lord Stormont, who was secretary of state, 1779–82.[36] Dundas wanted the role of Scottish manager. He also needed access to government patronage to build up Scottish support for the government and his own power base. Unsettled times followed. His career went on hold during the brief Rockingham administration. But in July 1782 under the Shelburne administration, he became officially recognised as manager of Scotland for the first time. Two other great rewards came to him under Shelburne. First, he was given life tenure of an office he had long coveted, the keepership of the Signet, which drew in very handsome fees, as well as being a source of patronage in the form of small offices. Second, Dundas formed a friendship with William Pitt when serving with Shelburne. Dundas lost office during the Fox-North coalition; but he continued to build up this friendship.

In December 1783 a small group, including Pitt, met at Dundas's house to plan the coalition's dismissal, which followed in the same month. Dundas's strength of character and his effectiveness in the Commons made him useful to the government. His burgeoning friendship with Pitt was also of great value to the prime minister. In the centre of government, at first with William Grenville (Pitt's cousin) and then alone, Dundas shared the burden of the war from 1793 and the lesser problem of the radical challenge with Pitt, 'every act of his being as much *mine as his*', said the prime minister.[37] Dundas's other great asset for the government was his role as Scottish manager. Regarding the latter, it is interesting that when Pitt, at the outset of his administration, handed Scotland and its patronage over to Dundas, (apart from retaining concern with revenue administration), it took time to build up a strong interest. Incidentally, the home secretary at the start of the administration, Lord Sydney, who was responsible strictly speaking for Scotland, caused no problems.[38]

The government received several rebuffs from the Scots and others, however, as Paul Kelly explains, at a time when Pitt was still a relatively inexperienced politician. There were difficulties in 1784–85. Pitt had to repeal his own cotton tax not long after its introduction, in the face of popular protests in Lancashire and Scotland, and also withdrew a tax on coal shortly after it was introduced. The Scottish opposition to the coal tax included his own supporters. Brown adds that there was a negative reaction from the Scottish political classes to the government's Irish proposals in 1785. Also in that year, the government plan to reorganise the court of session was rejected, an embarrassing rebuff. Such opposition was gradually overcome.[39] Dundas tirelessly continued to consolidate the government support in Scotland. A feature was the way he built up local alliances, most notably in the north and northeast in the late 1780s (Chapter 2). He then benefited from the outbreak of war in 1793, which discouraged opposition, and also from defections in the reformist Whig ranks in their response to the threat of radicalism. The general election of 1796 produced 43 loyal MPs from the 45 Scottish constituencies.[40]

There are two other features of the scene to mention – Indian patronage and Whig opposition to Dundas in Scotland. An aspect of Indian patronage was Dundas's anxiety that public opinion should not be outraged by the number of Scots benefiting from it, a subject of public comment. The key aspect, however, was that the board of control did not have power in East India Company appointments. Therefore the common assumption that Dundas used his position to increase his powers of patronage vastly in Scotland is wrong. Turning to the matter of the Whig opposition to Dundas, the three principal personalities in this were Henry Erskine, William Adam and Sir Thomas Dundas. Sir Thomas, the member for Stirlingshire and a rich man, was the son of Henry Dundas's old adversary, Sir Lawrence. He therefore had a background of animosity towards Henry Dundas (they were, incidentally, only very distantly related). He was also a sponsor, if hardly a champion, of parliamentary reform in Scotland and turned moderate in the face of the extra-parliamentary radicalism of the early 1790s. William Adam, member for the Elgin burghs and then Kincardineshire, was on friendly terms with Henry Dundas, but was opposed to him on fairly innocuous reformist grounds. Henry Erskine, who was not an MP, had been lord advocate during the Fox-North coalition. He shows no sign of liking Henry Dundas, but his motivation may, in any case, have been on ideological grounds as he had good reformist credentials. In terms of party structures, Sir Thomas Dundas, who had a parliamentary interest in Richmond, Yorkshire, as well as his substantial Scottish ones, was 'the principal intermediary between opposition interests in Scotland and England.'[41] William Adam was a man of business, becoming party manager of the Fox-Portland opposition towards the end of 1788. Henry Erskine led a group of politicians and lawyers who became the centre of opposition activity in Scotland – their representation at Westminster was small. Under Erskine's leadership, they founded the Independent Friends in 1785 to rally Whig opposition support in Scotland. The Fox-Portland group to which the Scottish Whigs were linked was opposed to Pitt on ideological grounds. Charles James Fox also bore strong personal animosity towards the King. The 'Foxite' Whig opposition came to focus round the Prince of Wales in the traditional way.

In the winter of 1788-9 the opposition provoked a crisis, the regency crisis, when the King was suffering an attack of porphyria. They raised the possibility of the King's permanent incapacity and succeeded in having a bill in the Commons which would give the Prince authority to act as regent without limitations. However the King recovered in time to prevent the bill passing in the Lords. The opposition aim had been the dismissal of the government by the Prince of Wales. As the alarm grew about the developing radical challenge outside parliament, however, the opposition's days as an effective force were numbered. Fox's defence of the French revolution split the movement. Henry Erskine began to campaign against the dangers of radical reform in 1792 (Chapter 7) and the Duke of Portland joined Pitt's cabinet in July 1794.

5

THE JACOBITES

This short chapter allows us to step back a bit from the activities of the political establishment. It provides a reminder of the Jacobite presence during the reigns of the first two Georges; and it deals with the strength of the commitment to Jacobitism in Scotland until it became a spent force after the '45. The concern is not, however, to spend time on the threat the Jacobites posed to the Hanoverian regime. The aim in considering the strength of Scottish Jacobitism is to emphasise that the ruling regime in Scotland did not have an overwhelming consensus on their side. The Jacobites were a substantial presence in Scottish life and, although the Whigs dominated politics in Scotland as in England from the accession of George I, political accord did not prevail throughout the community. During Ilay's time as manager, the people in power in the Scottish Hanoverian political elite dealt with unsympathetic elements by means of careful management, persuasion and the use of power where necessary. The resources of the state were great enough to keep Jacobitism in check in England and Scotland in peaceful times.

As for the challenge posed by the Jacobites and exiled Stuarts in times of 'emergency' – the term the authorities used when risings were threatened or in progress – this depended not simply on the Jacobites' potential support, but on their ability or otherwise to plan and co-ordinate their campaigns, get their supporters out and, above all, in the midst of all the twists and turns of French foreign policy and diplomacy, get adequate help from France in the form of invasion attempts, more substantial help that is than the modest contribution made by an ill-fated French naval squadron in 1708. The

Jacobites failed in these respects, but had they succeeded – for example if a French-supported Jacobite army including a substantial Scottish presence had entered London – the possible outcome remains a subject for ultimately fruitless debate.

In the literature on Jacobitism there are widely varying perceptions of the significance of the phenomenon and the challenge it posed to the post-revolution, post-union regime. The study of Jacobitism is a hazardous one. It is particularly susceptible to the vagaries of historical fashion and to passionately held views. Those who dismiss Jacobitism as a sideshow or disregard it tend to be categorised in a very general way, often unjustly, as following the old, so-called Whiggish view of history with its assumptions about 'the rise of parliament, the development of political parties and the growth of a more liberal and democratic society'.[1] On the other hand, one has to be no less alert to the use of Jacobite propaganda in the more recent debate about Scotland's nationhood. For example, the *Memoirs of Scotland* (published 1714), by the Jacobite polemicist George Lockhart of Carnwath, who attacked the motives of the Scots promoters of the union, has been used in support of the modern-day nationalist cause with little or no regard for Lockhart's partiality. Accurate though parts of Lockhart's analysis were, not least in highlighting the personal benefits that accrued to the union's champions, it did not accord with the contemporary pro-union Whig perspective of events. It has to be remembered that Lockhart's work contained a fierce propaganda element.

There was a strong ideological, even crusading, aspect to Scottish Jacobitism, but there were also worldly motives. The Stuarts had committed themselves to dissolving the union to help effect their restoration to their three kingdoms of England, Scotland and Ireland.[2] The union also perpetuated the revolution's church settlement, opposed by the great majority of Jacobites. And, finally, the union, together with the confirmation of the protestant succession in the house of Hanover upon George I's accession in 1714, assigned the Jacobites to the political wilderness, with the serious economic consequences and curtailment of freedoms that entailed. It was therefore in the very reasonable self-interest of Scottish Jacobites to attack the union; and when the latter was at the height of its unpopularity in the early years, they knew the value of negative rhetoric. This is not to deny that they had genuine ideological objections to the union. But there was a self-seeking element in Jacobite attacks, well understood by their opponents. The Jacobites knew well that the breaking of the union would help them accomplish their designs. Their polemic is now prone to be taken at face value.

Jacobitism was not only a force in Scotland. In a revisionist assessment, Eveline Cruickshanks estimates that all but a handful of the leading Tories in England at the time of the Atterbury plot (1722) were active Jacobites. Again, Ian Christie estimates that almost half of the members of the parliament of 1741 had Jacobite sympathies.[3] There were also people at the very centre of power in the latter years of Queen Anne, to wit Lords Oxford and Bolingbroke, willing to contemplate the accession of 'James III and VIII' to the throne. And before both the '15 and the '45, English Jacobite conspirators lobbied France to send expeditions to England in support of risings. But the signal failure of English Jacobites to rally to the cause in numbers or with any semblance of gritty determination in 1715 and 1745 – or, indeed, at any other time – is striking. This can be explained partly by failure to get the requisite level of French support and by other exigencies, including the circumstance that the risings which started in Scotland were not part of agreed strategies.

In 1715 the insurrection in the north of England was planned by Anglican Jacobites as part of a campaign in which the main thrust was to be in the south and involved the landing of French troops in the southwest. When this plan was thwarted, the end product was a rising in the north dominated by Catholic recusants. This ended in surrender at Preston. In 1744 and at the beginning of 1745, English Jacobites and Charles Edward Stuart pressed unsuccessfully for France to send an expedition to England. The English believed that a Scottish expedition would not succeed unless there was also a landing near London.[4] To a degree, therefore, the English failure to support Bonnie Prince Charlie when he took the initiative and sailed for Scotland is understandable. But although the muted support in England for the cause in the rebellions of 1715 and 1745 is explicable in such terms, the zeal of Scottish Jacobites is in such stark contrast that it merits comment. Ferreting out the sources of that strength will also help explain the nature of Scottish Jacobitism.

Jacobitism may have been given particular encouragement at an early stage in Scotland by the chance circumstance that Scots, the Earl of Melfort and the Earl of Middleton, were 'secretaries of state', chief advisers, in the exiled Stuart court in the formative years after the revolution. Indeed, they contributed to what Edward Gregg describes as the 'pernicious and endemic' national differences between the English, Scots and Irish there.[5] During the '15, the exiled Bolingbroke was the secretary of state in the Pretender's mock court, but was ousted in 1716 by the Earl of Mar. The latter was in turn ousted in 1724 by Colonel John Hay of Cromlix – son of the sixth Earl of Kinnoull – who had the faintly extravagant title of Earl of Inverness in the Jacobite peerage and became a duke when removed from office in 1727. Perhaps of more substance than the Scottish influence in the Pretender's court was the role of the Highlands in Jacobite campaigns.

The Highlands provided a remote strategic base in which to marshal support without intervention by the authorities; although a rather modest military presence – garrisons in the Great Glen and regular forces supported by local irregular companies – helped General Wightman to deal promptly with the incipient rising of 1719.[6] The strategic importance of the Highlands was recognised most obviously in the construction by General George Wade and his successors of military roads in support of the garrisons. More fundamental still in shaping Jacobitism's strong Scottish profile was the nature of Highland society. The long-held view has represented that society as a commercially backward one, in which the militant clan system provided the Jacobites with officers and fighting men. This view has come under attack, most persuasively in the work of Allan Macinnes. He explains that the militarism of the clans can be overplayed. In the eighteenth century there was no longer a military caste in clan society. The role of the tacksmen, who provided a link between the clan elite and the clansmen, was primarily managerial not military. The tacksmen were intermediaries between a landowning elite and the farming and labouring clansmen. No longer were feuds resolved by fighting, and banditry was the province of cateran bands not of the clans.

Macinnes discusses the growth of commerce and holds the view that clanship's priority, in a hostile Highland environment, was that the land should be peaceably and productively settled. A possible difficulty with his argument is that two of the apparently best-informed Whig leaders at the time of the '45, Archibald, Duke of Argyll (formerly Lord Ilay) and Lord Milton, his manager in Scotland, did not see matters in that way. Supported by Argyll, Milton (with General Humphrey Bland) framed the plan that led to the formation of the annexed estates commission with the intention of changing the old ways in the Highlands (see Chapter 6). Milton and Argyll also used the board of trustees for manufactures to promote development in the Highlands (although we might keep in mind that a perhaps disproportionate level of support from the trustees in the 1750s went to Argyllshire, which was already loyal to the regime). However, Argyll and Milton were not Highland gentlemen. The London-based Duke only succeeded to the Argyll title and estates in 1743, and may have been operating on the basis of common prejudices. Among a different set of factors Macinnes points to as shaping strong support in the Highlands for Jacobitism, one was the growth of Episcopalianism there between the Restoration and the revolution. He explains that Catholicism was also present, but struggled in the face of severe penal laws and perhaps contributed little more than 20 per cent of the Jacobite force mobilised during the risings. He argues that the advance of Episcopalianism was significant in that, complemented by the hierarchical structure of clanship, it inculcated a spirit of obedience to royal authority. There was a predisposition therefore to support the legitimacy of the Stuarts. Non-juring Episcopalians – in other words, those who would not take oaths of loyalty – constituted some 75 per cent of the Jacobite activists in the principal risings. In his caveats Macinnes observes that religion was not necessarily the prime determinant of Jacobite commitment, particularly as there were cases in which pro- and anti-Jacobite political allegiances cut across religious denominational lines. He therefore considers the broader context of dynastic and nationalist factors, including the impact of the union.[7]

At this point, however, it would be useful to pursue the Episcopalian theme and, in doing so, turn to the work of Murray Pittock. In his analysis of the Scottish Jacobites mobilised in the '45, Pittock joins Macinnes in challenging the old view of the Jacobites as belonging to an outmoded state of society. He points to Jacobite improvers and those with significant mercantile interests, and goes so far as to describe the Jacobite support as 'significantly middle class'. Pittock differs radically from Macinnes in one respect. He argues that the Jacobite army in 1745 was largely from the Lowlands. Only 43–6 per cent of the troops seem to have come from the Highlands. Highlanders predominated in the councils of war, but the leadership of the army was mainly in Lowland hands, as in 1715. And of 112 officers of 'field rank' or above in 1745 less than half were Highlanders, the Highland habit of attaching the rank of colonel to small retinues notwithstanding. The geographical base was widely spread, but the Jacobite Lowland heartlands matched traditionally strong Episcopalian areas almost exactly, particularly in the east of Scotland north of the Tay. Whether we are talking about the Highlands or the Lowlands, therefore, Episcopalianism is the strongest common factor in Scottish Jacobitism. Pittock assesses that those whose allegiance was Presbyterian had a 'secure majority' only south of the Tay and adds, contentiously, that over half the population lived north of it.[8]

The Episcopalianism from which Scottish Jacobitism drew much of its support not only represented an important section of Scottish society, it also defined Scottish Jacobitism's ideological basis. When that ideology was applied by Scottish Jacobites to the unfortunate predicament of Scotland – as they saw it – it can be argued that this gave their movement great purpose. Pittock cites a sermon preached in 1715 by Professor James Garden of Aberdeen as an example of the welding together of Episcopalian religious belief and condemnation of political events in Scotland. The union was viewed by Garden as one of the calamities that had been visited upon Scotland by God, in punishment for what happened at the revolution – the abolition of the ancient apostolic form of church government, the usurpation of the rights of the church by schismatic teachers, and disobedience to the monarch (who Episcopalians believed to have an indefeasible hereditary right). For these 'heinous Sins and Abominations of Rebellion, Injustice, Oppression, Schism and perjury', declaimed Garden, 'God in his just wrath hath visited and plagued us with a long, a bloody and expensive war, several years of famine and extraordinary Dearth, accompany'd with Epidemical diseases and a great Mortality . . . with the loss of the Liberty, privileges and independency of this our Ancient Kingdom . . .'

It was all the more satisfying for Episcopalian ideologues that they could condemn the Presbyterian usurpers for the part the latter took in what the Episcopalians saw as the betrayal of Scotland at the union. Presbyterianism was associated by the Episcopalians with loss of national liberty, Episcopalianism with its restoration.[9] Perhaps it is churlish to demur when historians take the matter further by identifying the Episcopalian/Jacobite cause as a nationalist one. This sectional interest, a minority one and with an important part of its support coming from Highland society – so different from that of the Lowlands – is difficult to equate with nationalism, much as the Jacobites believed themselves to be fighting for liberties and a patriotic ideal. The debate tends to give the Jacobites the moral high ground, but it is not unreasonable to point out that Scotland's Whigs were not without ambitions for their country (Chapter 6).

The more severe predicament of Scottish Episcopalians relative to that of non-jurors and High Anglicans in England finally defined the strength of purpose, the greater determination, or perhaps the greater desperation of the Scots relative to their co-religionists in England. The essential difference between the two countries was that the majority of English Jacobites were members of the established church, whereas the majority of Scottish Jacobites, the Episcopalians, had been forced out of the established Church of Scotland and marginalised. The persecution of Episcopalianism culminated in the burning of chapels by Cumberland's troops after Culloden. But in normal times the oppression they experienced was less severe, certainly less so than that which the small Catholic community suffered. After the revolution William sought compromise and an accommodation between Presbyterians and loyal Episcopalians; but he plumped for the Presbyterian form of church government in preference to the Episcopal one.

There was a measure of protection for Episcopalian ministers against the Presbyterian onslaught, above all in the Church Act of 1695, which gave royal protection to Episcopalian clergy in possession of churches who took the oaths of allegiance and assurance.[10] Then the Toleration Act of 1712, passed by a Tory-oriented regime, allowed the Episcopal communion to meet and assemble without any let, hindrance or disturbance, 'for the Exercise of Divine Worship, to be performed after their own Manner', with a proviso that congregations, if they thought fit, could use the liturgy of the Church of England. And under the regime of Walpole's Scottish political manager from 1725, Lord Ilay, the pro-Jacobite leadership in the Scottish nobility and gentry were treated moderately.

Nevertheless, the state of affairs was, in reality, dismal. In their religious lives the Episcopalians were dealt a severe blow by the Toleration Act. Yes it allowed them to worship after their own forms; but it prohibited them from doing so in parish churches. In other words, it confirmed the total exclusion of Episcopalian ministers from the Church of Scotland – it confirmed the triumph of the Presbyterian usurpers. Then it made Episcopalians subservient to the Presbyterian Church of Scotland by insisting that their births and baptisms be registered in the parish church and that they pay their tithes or other dues to their parish minister. And before ministers of the Episcopal congregations (and of the established church) could exercise their duties, they had to take oaths of allegiance and abjuration. These oaths, it should be remembered, made them swear allegiance to Queen Anne, abjure allegiance to the Pretender, and do the utmost in their power to 'support, maintain and defend' the Hanoverian succession. In the secular world matters were similarly far from satisfactory. This may be judged from the plight of the pro-Jacobite element in the Scottish nobility upon the accession of George I. Many of these people, who included the ragtag and bobtail of the peerage, lived in very difficult circumstances, excluded from public office and benefiting only from handouts, for example in exchange for their votes at the election of representative peers. There was no place for them even in the profession probably nearest to their inclinations and most suitable to their rank, the law. In Scotland the practice of the law was closed totally under Act 10 Anne, c. 2 to those who had not taken the oaths. The general situation in England for Anglicans who were sympathetic to the Jacobite cause was better.[11] Those most firmly committed to the belief that the authority of kings was derived from God, the non-jurors, left the church, established their own congregations and were excluded from public office. There were opportunities in England's diverse and prosperous economy for these gentlemen, however, in the law (though they were prevented under Act 13 Will. III, c. 6 from practising in court) and other professions and in all manner of business and trade, as City merchants, bankers and manufacturers. They could also join the navy – the army was more strictly controlled.

The great majority of pro-Jacobite Tory landed gentlemen, those who *were* willing to take the oaths, also suffered after the accession of George I. Few of them got into government, and they did not benefit from government patronage and offices. They were excluded from the army, the civil service, ecclesiastical livings in the gift of the crown and county lieutenancies, from positions as judges and KCs, and from government contracts and the directorships of great public companies. The Tory Church of England also faced problems. Above all, it had to stomach the imposition of Whig bishops upon it. This was done in William's reign, when ejected non-juring bishops were replaced. Whig bishops were also appointed systematically under George I, which affected the career prospects of the lower clergy. At first it contributed to the drift of High Anglican clerics towards Jacobitism and their disaffection increased when the Tories lost power upon George I's accession. However the purging of malcontents by the government and conciliatory efforts by High Churchmen meant that, by the early 1720s, allegiance to the Stuarts among the Anglican clergy could only survive outside the ken of the episcopal authorities.[12]

Yet, in the midst of all this misery, it must be remembered that Tories could sit in the Houses of Commons and Lords, provided they took the oaths (an obligation under Act 13 Will. III, c. 6). In the Commons they were backbenchers, forced into permanent 'country' opposition; but at least they were able to participate in the parliamentary debate on the running of the country, the conduct of war and the economy, and did so with vigour. It would be interesting also to assess the benefits to them in the mass of private legislation that was passed. In short, the pro-Jacobite element in England did suffer from discrimination and repression; but they did not suffer the same level of social, political and economic isolation as their counterparts in Scotland. The incentive in England to take part in rebellion was not as strong as it was in Scotland.

6

THE LEADERSHIP'S IDEAS AND ASPIRATIONS

The intention here is to look at the role of the Scottish political leadership in promoting the interests of Scottish society, the economy in particular. With two qualifications, it is not the concern to place matters in the context of long-term historical processes, in particular the development of enlightenment thought and the build up to the industrial revolution. The first qualification is that there is a need to question the place given to civic virtue in the study of eighteenth-century politics. The dubious antecedents of appeals to virtue by political opposition during the century have already been suggested above. The deliberate and successful manipulation of self-interest as a force for economic improvement in mid century, as shown in the way the British Linen Company was formed by Lord Milton – Lord Ilay's henchman in Scotland from the mid 1720s to 1761 – should cause further reflection. So should the political characteristics of the board of trustees for manufactures and the Royal Bank of Scotland, both founded under Ilay's guiding hand. The other qualification is that a natural progression may be observed between, at either end of the century, the economic benefits of the union and the commercial vision of Henry Dundas.

Four challenges arise in assessing the contributions of the political managers to Scottish society. First, the ideas that influenced these men can be hard to discover. Second, the politicians worked to Scotland's benefit in general ways not always identified in specific actions. Third, it was not in the character of the British parliament in the eighteenth century to promote the internal development of the national economy by vigorous intervention: there is a danger therefore of looking for more from the Scottish political leaders than the times allowed. In this last context, there may also have been a perception that the key thing needed to advance the Scottish economy had already been achieved in 1707, with the union. Fourth, as implied in the above remarks about virtue, the more powerful actions of benefit to the Scottish economy that emanated from the oligarchy tended to have narrow political characteristics, not least the objective of maximising power; but there could be real economic and social purposes as well.

The contents of private libraries are a tempting source when trying to uncover politicians' beliefs, but can mean little, especially in an age of bibliophiles. Fortunately, the Duke of Montrose, secretary of state 1715–16, left a clue to his reading when, in about 1709, he asked for certain books from his library in Glasgow to be sent to him in London. These included: 'what pieces his Grace has of Mr Lock's, his commentaries on St Pauls Epistles excepted', and Samuel Pufendorf's *De Jure Naturae et Gentium* (Montrose had an edition of 1698).[1] Gershom Carmichael (1672–1729), who was from 1696 a regent and then the first professor of moral philosophy at Glasgow University, where Montrose had been a student, was an influential commentator on Pufendorf.[2] The latter took a rather benign view of the natural law (being less harsh in his understanding of human nature than Hobbes), a law grounded on our need to advance from our natural state to form communities for mutual protection and sustenance. Montrose's time in power was so short and he was so insecure in the face of the challenge from the Campbell brothers, John, Duke of Argyll, and Archibald, Earl of Ilay, that his views on society and his philosophy of government are of little consequence.

The same cannot be said of Ilay – one of the two great political managers of the century. The magnificent library of this polymath is an impossible challenge. How can one pick from this treasure house or from elements in his education at Glasgow and Utrecht to represent the kernel of his thinking? A provocative guess as to the secret spring of his actions is hazarded in pointing to the small set of books in his library on the laws of chance, catalogued beside those on mathematics. Ilay was fond of maxims of this sort: 'In short all's a game and I'll play the cards: *selon le jeu, quelq fois on gagne and quelq fois on perd*; in the main good cards never lose at the long run . . . though I am very far from thinking that any consolation maxims are necessary for me at present; I leave that to my enemies.'[3] The view of Richard Scott is that Ilay loved the political system for its own sake.[4]

The other great manager, Henry Dundas, lived in a society that was becoming increasingly more complex; the range of his opinions was not consistent; and there are many observations about his views. As a young lawyer, he frequented two of Edinburgh's intellectual clubs, the Speculative and the Belles-Lettres. He got to know Adam Smith in later years and introduced him to the younger Pitt. Dundas, in his response to the radical challenge of the later years of the century was conservative (see Chapter 7). David Brown and Piers Mackesy observe that he was he was not motivated by ideology.[5] Outside the area of party and factional politics, however, he formed an exceptionally clear strategy on world trade, a strategy he pursued relentlessly. The conclusion is inescapable that Smith's *Wealth of Nations*, which Dundas is known to have read, influenced him in that respect. Another influence was Charles Jenkinson, who educated him in Indian affairs.[6] Jenkinson (Lord Hawkesbury, 1786, Earl of Liverpool, 1796), an expert in commercial and financial business who was 30 years Dundas's senior, joined Dundas in 1784 on the newly formed board of trade. In 1786 he became president of the reconstituted board and in 1791 he joined Dundas in the cabinet.

The ways in which the political managers worked in general to Scotland's benefit, not always revealed in specific actions, could have been intentional or accidental. The element of stability the managers provided in political relations with England allowed economic enterprise to flourish without unnecessary encumbrances. Ilay protected Scotland from the worst excesses of English interference by making himself valuable to successive ministries in providing them with a large block of supporters. Again, Ilay, who outside times of emergency was prepared to use or work with Jacobite sympathisers in support of his electoral objectives, helped reconcile the Scottish political nation to the Whig interest.[7] His impact in the House of Lords over six decades would also be worth investigating. A representative peer in 1707–13 and 1715–61 – from 1743 as Duke of Argyll – he was very active in the Lords. His was a dominant presence in Scottish business there, perhaps until 1756 when William Murray, newly appointed to the English office of lord chief justice of the King's Bench, entered the house as Lord Mansfield. In February 1722, Montrose reported joyously on Ilay's being bested by Lord Aberdeen in an appeal from Scotland in the case Allardice v. Allardice. The vote went against the motion put by Ilay. The latter, said Montrose, 'lookt like the d___l not being accustomed to meet with such rubs, for he finds that hereafter his law is no longer to pass for gospell.' George Lockhart of Carnwath reported to the Pretender some weeks later that Ilay formerly took it upon himself in the Lords 'to cut and carve in all Scots appeals as the sole oracle and dictator of the Scots law'; but that Aberdeen kept him 'within bounds' in that session and protected the interests of the Scottish Tories when they had any business there. There is no indication that Aberdeen, a representative peer from 1721 to 1727, got the better of him for much longer: Aberdeen could never prosper in opposition to him.

It may be added that Ilay and his brother, the second Duke of Argyll, were not just active in the House of Lords in matters affecting Scotland. Graham Townend, in dealing with 1715–22, notes their activity in discussions on 'religion, foreign policy, the national debt, elections, the threat of disease and the abuse of protests in the House of Lords'.[8] In the later decades of the century, Henry Dundas had such influence with Pitt as 'allowed him to protect Scots interests where these did not clash with English political or administrative requirements.'[9] He could go perhaps even further, by accident or design, in protecting Scotland, such was his strength. Thus the attention his interest gave to the Bank of Scotland and Royal Bank, the outcome of which was an informal affiliation between the banks for political ends, was at the centre of events indicating to London that Scotland had its own banking network and that the Bank of England had only a limited role north of the border.[10]

When judging the government and administration of post-union Scotland, the rather flimsy encouragement given to the Scottish national economy by successive administrations is, however, marked. There was perhaps some failure of leadership in comparison with what happened before the union. But the difficulties any politician faced in eighteenth-century Britain in trying to get state intervention in the encouragement of the Scottish economy have to be understood. In the seventeenth century, the increasing determination of the Scottish Privy Council and parliament to refashion the economy according to mercantilist principles is observed by Christopher Whatley. Structural weaknesses were tackled and Scottish enterprise was stimulated and protected.[11] Scotland's inherently weak position in competition with England, above all, made vigorous state intervention necessary.

I am among those who have fallen into the trap of assuming that the contrasting dearth of legislation after the union to encourage the Scottish economy as a whole meant that the interests of the country were being badly served by its politicians.

A qualification to this interpretation appears by looking at the legislative role of the British parliament. Much parliamentary time was taken up with the passage of private or local Acts (the latter appearing in The Statutes at Large among the public Acts until 1797). This conscious decentralisation by the government, in which it showed its receptivity to local, private and commercial needs and interests, did not mean that it was disinterested in advancing the national economy. The aim was to create the right conditions for enterprise to flourish, for example through attacking monopolies and combinations.[12] War with revolutionary France and an increasingly complex society and economy changed matters only towards the end of the century. There was then an increase in legislative activity of national scope.[13]

For many decades after the union, it was not practical in normal times for the Scottish leadership to introduce major national initiatives through legislation. Exceptions were the Acts of 1727 setting up and funding the board of trustees for manufactures, in response to continuing disquiet in Scotland about the imposition of the malt tax; and the Act of 1752 annexing the forfeited estates to the crown in the aftermath of the '45. Acts of such scope were very unusual because they were contrary to the philosophy of government in England at that time; but the alternative of private or local Acts could be beneficial. Alexander Murdoch cites four improvement Acts obtained for the city of Edinburgh; the first by Archibald, Duke of Argyll in 1754; another by Sir Lawrence Dundas in 1767, which extended the royalty of the burgh to cover the area on which the new town was built; and two more, by Henry Dundas in 1785 and 1786, leading to the construction of the university's old college and the South Bridge. Lawrence Dundas also worked in parliament on behalf of the Forth-Clyde canal project.[14] The patriotic principles of the grandees who obtained local Acts are not in question. Nevertheless, the fundamental inspiration of their support for such legislation was political. It was part of the exercise of patronage to maintain political interests. The only other qualifying comment is that a trawl of the lists of Acts in the reigns of the first two Georges shows that Scottish local legislation was not common in that period and was far outstripped by the mass of English local Acts.

Another justification for the lack of political activity on the economic front in the two decades up to 1727 is the perception that the union with England was the greatest encouragement imaginable to the Scottish economy, even allowing that the effects took decades to work through. The perception was triumphantly affirmed in the Scottish poet James Thomson's 'Rule, Britannia' (1740):

> To thee belongs the rural reign;
> Thy cities shall with commerce shine;
> All thine shall be the subject main,
> And every shore its circles thine.

In the second half of the century – and certainly to Henry Dundas – it was very obvious the union was valuable to the Scottish economy. A possible outcome of the union was the underdevelopment of the economy, through exposure without protection to England's economic might; but this did not happen. Instead, Scotland benefited greatly from its unhindered access to a free-trade area, that of England and, under the umbrella of the navigation Acts, England's colonies. The benefit was all the greater after the Peace of Utrecht in 1713 (at the end of the War of the Spanish Succession), which, though it could have achieved more, gave Britain colonial and commercial advantages and set the course to give it the leading position in world trade: if the union had not taken place, Scottish troops would have contributed to England's victories without sharing the commercial spoils. The consensus view is that, after a flat period, the Scottish economy began to perk up appreciably in the 1750s and 1760s. This is not just attributable to the union; but the union's economic benefits are undeniable. In relation specifically to the colonial trade, clandestine illegal commerce with the English colonies – an active trade before 1707 – would have been a poor substitute if the union had not happened. The trading environment would have been dislocated.

The importance to Scotland of the tobacco trade with the 13 American colonies is well known through the work of T. M. Devine. The great part of the trade was based on the re-export of the tobacco from the Clyde to Europe. In 1783 at the end the American War of Independence, the United States was freed from the shackles of the navigation laws. It may be imagined that the Scots could then, if the union had not taken place, have entered the trade unencumbered by English laws. The Scots would have been hard pressed to succeed, however, in the absence of well-established trading relations with the 13 colonies. As it was, the Scots benefited greatly from their American connections. This happened during the war, when the tobacco trade and the export of goods to the 13 colonies were rerouted through the West Indies and other channels of commerce; and after the war, when Scots factors returned in numbers to Virginia and established a direct trade with Europe.[15]

The other major colonial market which Scots commerce exploited in the eighteenth century was the West Indies. It is easy to overlook the commercial importance of the British West Indian colonies. Yet, for example, in 1784–86 they exported produce worth £4.5 million to Britain, when the latter's own domestic exports were no greater than £14 million. In the 1780s the re-export from Britain of West Indian produce accounted for 9 per cent of all exports. And in the same decade, investments in the West Indies accounted for 7–10 per cent of Britain's income. In the 1790s there were some 465 000 slaves on the British islands.[16] A perhaps surprising aspect of the big and varied trade between Scotland and the West Indies was the export of a significant portion of the Scottish fish catch to the islands. The first part of this trade was the export of cod and ling, mainly dried, much of this catch being from the Minch and off the coasts of Orkney and Shetland. Another part was the export of white herring (that is salted and unsmoked), a fair proportion of it from the northwest Highland fishery. The herring was not a true Scottish export as most of it went at a low price to Irish ports, such as Cork and was then exported to the West Indies by vessels, mainly English, trading with Ireland.[17] The Greenland whalers also contributed to the West Indian trade. The key to the fish trade was the supply of cheap food for the slaves. In emphasising the importance of the West Indies to Scotland Whatley gives the example of sugar and rum imports, which doubled between 1790 and 1815 in support of refineries and distilleries in Glasgow, Greenock and Port Glasgow. There were also opportunities for young Scots in the West Indies. India was even more important in that respect, providing openings for Scots in the service of the East India Company and, in numbers disproportionate to those from England, in trading on their own account. The benefit to the economy of Scotland from the connection with India arose not so much from trade as from the fortunes made and the remittances sent home.[18]

The reluctance of parliament to intervene in directing the national economy meant, as explained, that major economic initiatives affecting

Scotland were few and far between. And the obtrusively political nature of the regime at Westminster and of the Scottish management tended to give such initiatives a strong political character except in special circumstances. The founding in 1714 of the commission of police – a board which set out with a remit including specific public improvements and which quickly became merely a source of patronage through the salaries paid to its commissioners – is a crude example of the political aspects of innovation. The politics behind the two major initiatives of 1727, the establishment of the board of trustees for fisheries and manufactures and of the Royal Bank of Scotland, were altogether more intense and subtle. These bodies were set up just two years after Ilay became the political manager of Scotland, following his success in dealing with the malt-tax disturbances. The founding of the board of trustees and the Royal Bank tends to be associated with the zeal of polite society in Scotland for public improvement. However, people in Scotland did not have the clout to get such measures introduced simply as benevolent Acts. The board of trustees owed its being to an initiative in 1726 by the political management in London.

This initiative was in response to continuing discontent in Scotland with the malt tax. The discontent was expressed particularly in petitions of 1725 and early 1726 from the convention of royal burghs. In response a scheme was put together in London and transmitted to Edinburgh secretly.[19] The intention was that it was to be returned to London by the standing committee of the convention of royal burghs as if emanating from them. It would then be approved in London, and indeed it was. The scheme was that sums owing to Scotland should be handed over to disinterested persons (the trustees) to be used for the encouragement of manufacturing. These sums were due to the Scottish public under the arising equivalent and Acts of 1718 and 1724 in compensation for losses incurred at the union. The logic of the scheme was that a favourable response from the ministry to the petition from the royal burghs would give Ilay and Walpole great political credit in Scotland and stabilise things there without being seen in Westminster as caving-in to Scottish demands. It may be added that the board of trustees was dominated by Ilay's placemen and it stayed in the vicelike grip of their leader, Milton, until the early 1760s. In this it was an extension of Ilay's political hegemony in Scotland.

The Royal Bank, established by royal charter, was, of course, a financial institution; but its background was strongly political and it displayed political aspects into the 1740s and again from the 1760s. The political context of its early years is found in a remark by Robert Wodrow, writing in 1730, that the Duke of Argyll and Ilay were taking 'much pains to have some interest in all the various societies of Scotland and to have some thorough engaged to their side every where'.[20] The second Duke of Argyll and Ilay, the latter in particular, were determined to control the mechanisms of political patronage and to impose their own order where they could. Their political tendency was monopolistic. In 1705 there had been a sign of things to come. At that time the Scottish economy was suffering from a dearth of specie. The financial guru John Law argued in 1705 that this was partly because the Bank of Scotland had encouraged the export of coin. Law proposed that the bank should be taken over by parliament and be incorporated into a new national bank. The alternative he proposed was the reconstruction of the bank. This, explains Richard Saville in an important interpretation, would have involved a confiscatory statute. What lent Law's proposals authority was the power of his patron, the young Duke of Argyll (who had a strong political interest and was the Queen's commissioner to parliament in that year). Argyll's interest would have gained a major say in the supply of Scottish credit if either of Law's proposals had gone through. Fears of this, Saville remarks, led to the rejection of the scheme by parliament.[21]

After the union Argyll and Ilay retained a strong interest in banking and finance. The Bank of Scotland was too broadly based to be subject to their control, but it was still vulnerable to attack. It was also dangerously associated with their enemies, the squadrone. Ilay's first obvious excursion into currency schemes came in 1719–20 when he visited Paris and got his fingers burnt in the disastrous failure of Law's Mississippi scheme, the French equivalent of the South Sea Bubble. It is said that he also invested in the scheme on behalf of his friend Henrietta Howard, sometime mistress of the Prince of Wales (the future George II), and possibly even on behalf of the Prince himself. Ilay also speculated in the South Sea stocks in London. On 30 September 1720 – at the time of the collapse of the bubble, when 'multitudes of people' were 'ruined and undone' – Ilay attended a general court of the South Sea Company. His banker and close friend, George Middleton, goldsmith in the Strand, reported the next day that: 'There was like to have been great confusion at the Court, which was prevented coming to the greatest disorder by a speech My Lord Ilay made there and for which he is much applauded by every body here.'[22]

Middleton (the successor of John Campbell, the goldsmith who started the business in the Strand in 1692), Argyll and Ilay also had important Scottish financial interests. They and some of their associates were among substantial holders of debentures – in which there was a trade – issued in lieu of payment to those who had claims on the arising equivalent. In 1719 the debenture holders failed in an attempt to have themselves incorporated under royal charter as the 'Society of the Subscribed Equivalent Debt'. This would have enabled them to operate as a bank. Saville makes the point that the scheme could have sunk the Argyll interest; because – judging from other financial activities at the time of Middleton, Patrick Campbell of Monzie, Argyll and other leading financiers of the equivalent – they would have embarked at the very height of the London boom upon a stockjobbing exercise for speculative purposes. It was only in 1724, however, by which time Argyll and Ilay were closely allied to the head of the administration, Walpole, that an Act was passed incorporating the holders of the debentures into the Society of the Equivalent Company. The debentures, face value £248 550, were the company's capital. The company was restricted to collecting and dispersing £10 600, paid by the government in annual interest and administrative costs on the debentures.

In 1727 Argyll and Ilay achieved their next objective when the company was granted a royal charter allowing it to operate as a bank. It became the Royal Bank of Scotland. People in London held most of the debentures, the bank's capital. Many of these people were not Scottish. It is useful to mention this in emphasising that the new bank was, first and foremost, a financial body. But there was also a strong political element inextricably linked with the financial one. The channelling of Scottish public and army revenues through the Royal Bank was one sign of this. There was also a strong party or factional aspect until the early 1740s, symbolised by the appointments of the squadrone peers Marchmont and Tweeddale, Ilay's enemies, as governors of the Bank of Scotland in 1728 and 1742 respectively, and Ilay's appointment as the first governor of the Royal Bank. There was ferocious competition between the banks in the early years. The struggle was all the more intense because of the Royal Bank's weak cash base when it started out; and its misfortune in being founded in the year of a poor harvest, which was followed by a 'great scarcity of money' in 1728.[23]

Narrow political considerations came to the fore again in the 1760s, as Saville describes. These were marked by Sir Lawrence Dundas's appointment as governor of the Royal Bank in 1764. He and his supporters on the board used influence to favour his political interest in the bank's lending policy. In 1774 his opponent Henry Dundas (deputy governor of the Bank of Scotland from 1775) and some members of the board began to buy up Royal Bank shares. As a result, Sir Lawrence stood down as governor, being replaced by Henry's close political friend, the Duke of Buccleuch. In broader political terms, it was Henry Dundas's intention that both banks should function as part of the government interest and therefore his own. The consequence was, explains Saville, that they formed the largest source of potential credit controlled by any political group in eighteenth-century Britain.[24]

Two initiatives by Lord Milton in mid century arose from his influential position in looking after the Scottish end of the political management on behalf of Ilay (who was by then Duke of Argyll). These initiatives, despite such political ramifications, were essentially directed towards the development of Scottish society. One of them led to the establishment of the British Linen Company. The other proposed dramatic intervention in Highland society after the '45 and led to the establishment of the annexed estates commission. Milton and General Humphrey Bland, the new commander-in-chief in Scotland, submitted the latter scheme to the government in late 1747. Milton was particularly in favour at the time because of the great help he had given to the government during the '45. His proposals for the Highlands – it is hard to give any real acknowledgement to the role of Bland, a comparative novice – are now perhaps only of passing interest. At the time the scheme was proposed, Highland society was already changing through the working of time; through the mortal blow to Jacobitism struck at Culloden and in its terrible aftermath; and through the abolition of a source of arbitrary power in the Highlands, the heritable jurisdictions. There were also delays in the scheme's implementation even in limited form, by which time Milton was old and frail. And his dramatic plan to place a great part of the central Highlands in the hands of the government, or – more precisely – in the hands of a commission in Edinburgh (a commission which would of course be in his control) was watered down in the Annexing Act of 1752.

The intention had been not only to have the forfeited estates of rebels annexed to the crown, but also for the government to purchase swathes of land in rebellious areas. This would have dispelled the power of the chiefs forever. But, unsurprisingly, the interventionist plan to purchase lands was delayed and then lapsed. His declared purpose, which in retrospect seems to have had a dated feel to it even when it was proposed, was to bring permanent peace to the disaffected Highlands by attacking the role of the chiefs and their tacksmen. It stands in stark contrast to Allan Macinnes's analysis of the Highland economy, referred to in Chapter 5 above. Milton's view, or at least the bleak view of things he preached to a receptive audience, that is to the Duke of Newcastle, the secretary of state responsible for Scotland, was that the chiefs, whose prosperity and security depended upon the number of fighting men at their disposal, deliberately kept the population in ignorance and poverty to maintain control. So the chiefs discouraged 'all attempts to introduce the knowledge of the protestant religion and our happy constitution, and the true notions of husbandry, trade, and manufacture'. The tacksmen, whom he called duniewassels, the officer class the chiefs depended upon, had 'been successful instruments to keep the common people in slavery'. The tacksmen also thought themselves to be 'of too high blood to stoop to trade and manufacture'. And, in general, the prevalent attitudes made 'the common people believe that they were the property of the chiefs'. Only when the power of the chiefs had been removed could the introduction of other measures, such as the encouragement of industry, be successful.[25]

Milton devised the British Linen Company – or, more correctly, the Edinburgh Linen 'Copartnery' as it was before being granted a royal charter in 1746 – to promote the Scottish economy, but without any appeal to public spirit. Christopher Smout, in reviewing the first three quarters of the century, refers to the significance of this banking venture and explains its purpose of relieving the liquidity problems of the linen industry and assisting in sales and marketing. He also describes it as 'a characteristic product of the age of improvers'.[26] Milton himself was a product of that age; but this need not imply that there was a kind of feeble virtue in his character. Improvement came out of hard-headed ideas. In 1744 he explained the way in which his 'Grand Manufactory' would work:

> I have lived long enough to see that in private as well as public treaties mankind will be no further bound than they find their interest leads them – one way or other they'll declare off, and pursue what they think most for their interest. This led me to contrive a copartnery so that the good of the whole might become the particular private interest of each person any way con-

cerned in the management. After all that's commonly said of public spirit we in fact see that 'tis private interest that makes every person active and diligent, opens his eyes and his ears, raises his invention, supports him under fatigue and makes his business an entertainment.

The two managers of the company were to be shareholders, not mere hirelings. They were to suffer from the losses and benefit from the profits. 'No purchase no pay shows a spirit', said Milton: the bait of a share in the profits 'adds grease to the wheels and makes the whole machine work in good order'.[27] Bernard Mandeville wrote in his poem of 1705, 'The Grumbling Hive':

> Bare Virtue can't make Nations live
> In Splendor; they, that would revive
> A Golden Age, must be as free,
> For Acorns, as for Honesty.

Adam Smith wrote in *The Wealth of Nations* (1776): 'But man has almost constant occasion for the help of his brethren, and it is in vain for him to expect it from their benevolence only. He will be more likely to prevail if he can interest their self-love in his favour, and show them that it is for their own advantage to do for him what he requires of them.' Milton's manipulation of self-interest contrasts with the ideals of the 'civic tradition' (a term coined by J. G. A. Pocock) in Scottish political thought. Those ideals hearkened back to intellectual concepts developed to their fullest in sixteenth-century Florence on the role of the citizen in the city state. A most valuable analysis of the civic tradition's link to a preoccupation of eighteenth-century Scottish society is found in John Robertson's *The Scottish Enlightenment and the Militia Issue*. It is not possible here to do justice to his arguments or to the wider debate on the civic tradition. But, in the present context, two elements in the Florentine concept of the virtuous citizen stand out. The first was the perception that corruption, the rejection of the pursuit of virtue, occurred when citizens put their private, material interest before the public good. The second was that the citizen needed to display virtue by taking up arms whenever required, in other words, by participating in the militia: the value in such service was not just the defence of the country, for which an army of mercenaries would have sufficed, but in the unifying function it served in the community. The commitment before the union of Andrew Fletcher of Saltoun to a militia was in this civic tradition. In his writings Fletcher sought a federal union in which Scotland could establish a social order based upon civic principles in place of the old feudal inheritance. In this new order, he believed, his militia would be 'as great a school of virtue as of military discipline'.[28] The plan for the British Linen Company by Fletcher's nephew, Milton, was in a very different tradition, but was no less concerned with advancing the interests of Scotland. It was based on a living, dynamic idea. He was an influential politician; and his scheme came to fruition. In comparison, civic virtue in post-union politics, was, if judged on the basis of the militia issue, a wan and inconsequential thing. Not only did the agitation for a Scottish militia during the Seven Years' War and the American War of Independence fail, it was not within the true civic tradition. The moderate literati, who championed the militia cause, did not have intellectual values of that tradition. Whereas Fletcher saw the militia as providing an institutional framework in which Scots could affirm their citizenship, the moderates looked to it as merely providing a moral commitment. They looked simply to the diffusion of martial values.[29]

At the end of the century came the most graphic demonstration of all – by Henry Dundas – of the power of political influence combined with a clear, single-minded purpose. The circumstances also symbolised how Scotland had, by the century's end, become truly part of Great Britain, participating to the full in the economic union with England. The matter in question was Dundas's role at that time, which Michael Fry describes daringly, even provocatively, as that of the architect of the 'second British Empire, the Empire of trade'.[30] Mackesy describes how a pivotal point of achievement for Dundas came in 1800 when, as secretary for war and one of the triumvirate with Pitt and Grenville, the three 'efficient ministers', Dundas's views predominated in the cabinet in a clash with Grenville, the foreign secretary, over the purpose of the war. Although Pitt was the real decision-maker as controller of the purse, Dundas was successful in arguing against Grenville's emphasis on the need to overthrow the French government in Paris. Given the limited resources to fight the war, Dundas looked to a shift in emphasis from Continental warfare to a strategy which used the war to protect and advance Britain's real interests. His long-held view, which finally prevailed, was that: 'We are a small spot in the ocean without territorial consequences, and our own power and dignity as well as the safety of Europe, rests on our being the paramount commercial and naval power of the world.' The objectives were the consolidation and security of Britain's naval power and the conquering of markets, not territory.[31]

7

REACTION AND RADICALISM

The Church

Sir William Bennet of Grubbet wrote in 1725: 'Never was there such a spirit of rebellion, against all order and government as rages universally in this country.'[1] This was in the wake of a riot and popular clamour in the parish of Morebattle. The tumult was occasioned by the objection of the elders and congregation of the parish to the induction of a new minister, who had been presented to the parish by its 'patron' the Duke of Roxburghe. This is an example of a divide that existed between the landed elite and the common people throughout the century. The language used seems to be so ideological as to come from a later age; and it suggests not only assumptions of social superiority, but also a sense of anxiety and helplessness in the face of a threat from below. References of this sort are not commonplace outside the last couple of decades of the century, however, and present an exaggerated view of attitudes before then. Bennet's devotion to the bottle may help explain his paranoia. In general, the aristocracy and gentry were rightly complacent about their place in society during the century. Not until the 1790s did they feel there was a mass challenge from below along the lines suggested by Bennet. And they were able to deal with it. The extra-parliamentary radical challenge in the last two decades of the century represented the aspirations of a developing, increasingly complex and well-informed society for greater political participation and an end to 'the old corruption'. Only the extreme minority of those seeking change envisaged the overthrow of the old order in the French manner.

Although there were nervous times in the 1790s, the regime was not under serious threat at any time in the century – leaving aside opportunities for a major French-supported challenge from the Jacobites, something which never quite happened. But during the course of the century, even before the special problems of the radical years, the ruling order had to react to two troublesome problems from below. It could live with these, but they were only partly manageable. First, there was the problem of the church; and, second, there was the problem of riots and disturbances – in crude terms the problem of 'the mob'.

The Church of Scotland was a challenge because it was a relatively democratic institution within a non-democratic political order, and also because state interference in its affairs was contradictory to the powerful theological tradition, held sacred by the successors in spirit of the covenanters of the previous century. The Presbyterian form of church government did not recommend itself automatically to William of Orange before the revolution. He did not have a clear knowledge of the religious divisions that had rent Scotland, but what he saw he did not like. He hoped for compromise, a 'comprehensive' church settlement embracing the Presbyterian and Episcopalian traditions. Instead, he accepted reality in 1690 when the Presbyterian form of church government was restored. The reality was that the Presbyterians were the dominant party; they had bitter memories of their suffering under the bishops since 1661; and they were the party who would support William's regime.[2]

The restored Presbyterian Church of Scotland could never have an entirely comfortable relationship with the political regime of the eighteenth century. The church's democratic tendency was represented in its structure of government, a hierarchy of courts – the kirk sessions, presbyteries, synods and general assembly. The system continues to this day, except in that synods were abolished in 1992. Another important difference from today is that, in the eighteenth century, the church was a dominant local presence in the parish. It could, for example, interfere in the lives of individuals in matters of moral behaviour. The congregation in each parish elected ruling elders. These, with the minister ('the teaching elder'), acted as the kirk session, a body that governed at parish level. Each kirk session sent elders and its minister to the presbytery of the district. One of the presbytery's functions was to act as a court of appeal from the kirk sessions. Representatives went from the presbyteries to the provincial synod. And, more importantly, the presbyteries sent commissioners to the general assembly, the church's supreme court, which met in Edinburgh in May.

This system did not live easily with the non-democratic principles of the post-revolution political regime, which were reflected in the Whig-dominated politics of the eighteenth century. The exclusion of popular democracy was suggested in John Locke's *The Fundamental Constitutions of Carolina* (1669). Locke envisaged rule by a hereditary nobility and landed gentlemen under a nominal monarchy, 'that we may avoid erecting a numerous democracy'.[3] Moreover, the Presbyterian church's spiritual independence was a source of disharmony between church and state: there were two kings and two kingdoms, as Andrew Melville reminded James VI in 1595. The church recognised the secular authority of the state. Those who subscribed to the national covenant of 1638 swore to defend the King in the preservation of the 'true religion, liberties, and laws of the kingdom'. But to the zealous, state interference in the church's affairs was unacceptable. The Church of Scotland was the established church, but its head was Christ not the king.

At no time after the Glorious Revolution were those in the political elite willing to accept the stance of the religious zealots on the complete separation of the spiritual from the secular; although there was scope for concessions on political grounds. Similarly, landed society in general was equally keen to preserve its rights in church matters, specifically the right of lay patrons to present ministers to parishes; although, again, individuals sometimes made concessions and some landed proprietors were themselves of a zealous spiritual disposition. Patronages were *the* recurring flashpoint in the clash between the spiritual and the secular, but they were only part of the regime's problem in coping with the spirit of independence in the church.

The attitude of the political managers to the church during Ilay's long regime was expressed by his aide in Scotland, Lord Milton, in 1731: 'No society of men can subsist without doing good or bad, and since (whatever they may do in their private capacity) they can't do much good as a society, we should compound for their doing as little harm.'[4] In dealing with the church the political managers' first aim was to influence the general assembly. They could never entirely control it. The regime's most obvious defender in this respect was the royal commissioner who represented the monarch at the assembly. The commissioner was a nobleman uninvolved in the general political management. A letter to the assembly from the King supported him. This, essentially, gave assurances of royal favour if moderation prevailed in proceedings. And the commissioner came to the assembly armed with two sets of written instructions. These became ritualised with only occasional changes over the years. One set was for general consumption. A key aspect was the insistence that the assembly should do nothing to prejudice the royal authority or prerogative. To put this another way, there should be no interference with the rights of the state. Equally the commissioner had to take care that the assembly did not deal with anything that was an unfit subject for an ecclesiastical meeting.

The other set of instructions, the private ones (probably never intended to be kept secret), contained minor concessions to the church. One concession was that, notwithstanding other instructions, 'you may allow the assembly to approve the synod books, provided it be not mentioned in the assembly that these synod books contain any act ascertaining the intrinsic power of the church.'[5] The commissioner himself was subject to political guidance when at the assembly, certainly during Ilay's political regime. In 1724 Ilay advised Milton, his newly appointed assistant, that the commissioner, Lord Findlater, would 'want management, that is advice and encouragement'. And Ilay is recorded as 'epistolizing' the commissioner on troublesome matters identified by Milton.

Another feature of the management of the assembly during Ilay's regime, one that was evident in the 1720s and early 1730s, was the use he and Milton made of people who were representatives to the assembly from the royal burghs. Some of Ilay's most active agents, people conveniently resident in the Edinburgh area, represented individual burghs at the convention of royal burghs; agents including George Drummond, provost of Edinburgh, Patrick Lindsay, also sometime provost of Edinburgh (and a delegate to the convention from St Andrews), and George, master of Ross, delegate for Tain, Ross-shire. There was also scope for them to act as burgh delegates to the general assembly. Their role deserves further research. However, a convenient glimpse of the work such men could do in the assembly appears in 1732, thanks to one of Milton's rare trips to London. His absence meant that matters were dealt with by letter rather than in private conversation. George Ross advised Milton that James Alston should not be encouraged in his ambitions to be elected moderator that year.

Alston, an influential clergyman associated with Ilay's interest, had been showing rebellious tendencies. Ross wrote that it would 'not be thought proper to encourage Mr Alston to think himself absolutely necessary; he may indeed be very useful, when he comes to think right of himself and others.' Milton, no doubt after conversation with Ilay, instructed Ross to tell the royal commissioner, Lord Lothian, that Alston was to be opposed and that Neil Campbell, principal of Glasgow College, was the choice for moderator: 'your commands will be obeyed', replied Ross. Two loyal and immensely influential ex-moderators, William Hamilton and James Smith, were also instructed from London to support Campbell, who was duly elected.[6]

Such important churchmen of moderate persuasion who fought off the challenge from the zealots received rewards from the politicians in the form of presentation to desirable parishes, royal chaplaincies and university appointments. This tends to obscure the fact that these leading moderates had their own agenda to fulfil. It is true they did not have the stature of the great independent figure, William Robertson, the leading moderate in the assembly from the 1750s until his retirement from the business of the church courts in 1780. But they were in the same tradition, in upholding the law of the land in church affairs, in deflecting more severe state interference in the church, and in opposing zealotry. It would not go amiss to remember that Robertson developed into a great independent figure after having received his ample share of rewards from the politicians in the late 1750s and early 1760s. He had his first great success in the assembly in 1752 in persuading it to insist upon the presbytery of Dunfermline's responsibility to induct an unpopular presentee to the parish of Inverkeithing. The presbytery had failed, through the deliberate non-attendance of some of its members, to get a quorum to do this. In consequence of the assembly's hard line, one of those who absented themselves, Thomas Gillespie, minister of Carnock, a man fixedly opposed to civil interference in the church, was deposed.

William Hamilton, an unfashionable figure in enlightenment studies, was one of the important early influences on moderatism. Hamilton (1669–1732) was professor of divinity at Edinburgh from 1709 until his death. He taught a vast number of students. One of these, James Oswald, of the common-sense school of philosophy, said that many leaders of the church had 'been directed by the sentiments and spirit of Principal Hamilton whose scholars many of us were'. Hamilton was the son of a covenanter, yet was of liberal principles, disliking extremes.

He retained his affection for the covenanters yet taught a gentler, more conciliatory creed. He had the merit, wrote Ramsay of Ochtertyre, 'of breeding a number of eminent and amiable ministers who kept equally clear of fanaticism and laxity'. Hamilton co-operated with the politicians, as did two of the leading moderates of the next generation, whose work has been researched by Henry Sefton.

One was Robert Wallace. He rejected the zealot stance in that he recognised both the civil and ecclesiastical authority in the church. Following the suspension and deposition of John Glas, minister of Tealing, who rejected the authority even of church courts, Wallace said: 'We think these courts have not only the sanction of the law but also authority from Jesus Christ whereas he thinks all their authority is provided under the law of the land.' In fact, Wallace disliked patronages, but thought that belief in the people's divine right to elect their ministers' was wrong. Patrick Cuming was another conciliator who sought to mitigate relations between church and state. He is best remembered, however, for his role as Ilay's adviser and agent in church affairs for many years and for his management of the imposition of patronages, while his intellectual dullness makes him readily forgettable.[7] The leading clergymen employed by the political managers over the years included William Hamilton, James Smith, Neil Campbell and Patrick Cuming, who were used by Ilay; Robert Wallace, who was used by the squadrone secretary of state, Lord Tweeddale; and George Hill, Henry Dundas's adviser. The first two of these were linked to the squadrone before joining Ilay.

Lay patronage in the presentation of ministers to parishes generated much heat and noise, and was the key area in the dispute over secular interference in the church. At first sight, it seems surprising that patronage was dropped in the revolution church settlement of 1690 and was not revived until 1712. Patrons' rights were, after all, a form of property. The King also wished to preserve them. The Act abolishing the patrons' right of presentation was passed in July 1690 at the behest of the Earl of Melville, who was Scottish secretary of state and the King's commissioner to the Scottish parliament. This, however, was not entirely a concession to religious zeal. The circumstances have been analysed by Laurence Whitley.[8]

Melville aimed to undermine an aggressive coalition of selfish opposition interests in parliament, called 'the club'. The latter attacked the administration, with the aim of undermining those who had gained royal preferment. The club included people from divergent religious backgrounds. Despite this, it was united in calling for the abolition of patronages – a popular high Presbyterian cause – to embarrass the administration. To buy peace at a critical time for William's regime, Melville conceded the point to the club. The terms of the Act of parliament were leavened, however, by giving a place to heritors in the new arrangements. The nomination of ministers to fill vacancies was put in the hands of elders and heritors. These nominations were then to be submitted to the congregations for approval. A final say was given to the presbytery in cases where the congregation disagreed with a nomination. The heritors were local landowners who had responsibilities – shaped in part by legislation of the 1690s – for the provision and upkeep of church property, the payment of stipends, the provision of schools, and a role in the funding of poor relief. Among the heritors were lairds and landed magnates. In short, lay involvement in the spiritual affairs of the church continued. Trouble and dissension followed between 1690 and 1712 therefore, not least as a result of disputes between elders and heritors. In the second half of the century the selection of ministers by elders and heritors was, nevertheless, to become the favoured option of the leading anti-patronage group then in the Church of Scotland, the group known as the evangelicals or popular party, who were not truly in the old zealous tradition.

Patronages were restored by Act of parliament during the administration of Robert Harley, Lord Oxford. The pressure for change came from Scottish Tories. Oxford was dependent on the latter, whose sympathies were Episcopalian and usually Jacobite. The resumption of patronages benefited such Tory landowners by restoring their property rights and offering opportunities for the appointment of parish ministers of a relatively amenable disposition. There are signs that these so-called Tories also had a hidden purpose in pressing for the return of patronages. In Whitley's assessment they aimed to heighten the dissatisfaction of Presbyterians with the union and, thereby, enhance the appeal of the Pretender through holding out the prospect that he would dissolve it. The Duke of Argyll, who was not a Tory, intervened successfully in the House of Lords to have an amendment made to the bill in order to ensure that presentees would be Presbyterian. His brother Ilay voted against the bill, although privately declaring he was in favour of it, notes Whitley. To help understand Ilay's behaviour, I should add that the brothers always liked to portray the Argyll family as having a traditional role as champions or protectors of the church. This alluded back to the Marquis of Argyll's role as a leader of the covenanters. It was a useful posture for Argyll and Ilay politically. But these brothers, like the generality of the Scottish Whigs, found it easy to tolerate the restoration of patronages, no matter what Tory, Episcopalian or Jacobite measures had inspired the change. When Ilay became political manager of Scotland in 1725, he insisted vigorously on the rights of patrons being upheld. He did not accept the church's right to non-interference in its affairs by the secular authorities. After all, secular power had brought about the Presbyterian church settlement of 1690, from which all else followed.

An important consideration for Ilay and the other political managers of the century was that the crown was patron of perhaps a quarter of the parishes in the country. Other patrons included local landowners, the royal burghs and universities. The crown's role as a patron made a valuable contribution to the body of political patronage available to the managers. But this had its problems in the local disturbances that could take place when unpopular presentees were forced upon parishes. Compromises resulted. During the regimes of Roxburghe and Tweeddale, two of the squadrone secretaries of state, it seems that the business of crown presentations was handled cautiously. Thus Sefton describes how Robert Wallace, in advising and assisting Tweeddale in 1742–46, believed that 'the managers for the crown' should be given advice on the inclinations of 'those whose interest is likely to have greatest weight in bringing about comfortable and peaceable settlements'. In particular, Wallace took trouble to discover the inclinations of the heritors, elders and congregation when there was a vacancy.[9]

In Roxburghe's case there are inconsistencies. He insisted upon his private rights as a patron, as the Morebattle case shows, but was willing to compromise as secretary of state. In 1717 during his tenure in office, 1716–25, he and squadrone colleagues in London gave a sympathetic hearing to a church delegation, led by the influential minister William Mitchell, seeking the repeal of the Act of 1712. However, the initiative was baulked by Argyll and Ilay, who had authority even in opposition as they then were. They would not accept the change.[10] Ilay's regime as manager over two long spells, 1725–42 and 1746–61, was marked not so much by brutal determination, however, as by most painstaking management by Milton, Ilay and their close associates and clerical advisers. Candidates for presentation might be assessed in terms of: first, representations and recommendations received from interested parties; second, the political benefits to Ilay's interest; third, the ability and worth of the candidates; and fourth, the local appeal of the latter.

A qualifying comment needs to be added that Ilay's management of church patronage required the efficient compliance of a succession of English secretaries of state who had official responsibility for this Scottish business, in particular the Duke of Newcastle. This meant that Ilay did not have total control in managing crown patronage. Henry Dundas's approach was to defer to local landowners, preferring to intervene only when disagreements arose between them.[11] The managers' difficulties were eased by secessions from the church of those who were most against secular interference. The main secessions of the century took place in 1733 and 1761, led by Ebenezer Erskine and Thomas Gillespie respectively. Seceders did not form a threat to civil authority in church affairs because their meetings tended to be introspective, concerned with finances and religious and moral matters within their congregations. However, as will be seen, their anti-state tenets provided a breeding ground for late-century radicalism outside the church.

Richard Sher and Alexander Murdoch argue that the greatest anti-patronage unrest was displayed when the politicians were at their most conciliatory or unclear in their policies. At such times, there was hope of relief from patronages and so agitation and disputed presentations increased. From the mid 1780s, the patronage issue quietened down as frustration and apathy grew in a very unsympathetic political climate. The popular party also helped the regime in the 1790s, dissociating itself from radical activity. David Brown takes a rather different line. He observes that Henry Dundas, in retrospect, attributed the more peaceful environment within the church to his own patronage policy. Dundas's evenhandedness towards the heritors had the effect of answering some of the evangelical demands. Brown also refers to a meeting in Edinburgh at the end of 1792 between Dundas and the leading evangelicals, at which a truce was agreed in the church struggle. And he points to the perception of the political classes of the hold the clergy had over their congregations. This was an important consideration for Dundas. The clergy were seen as 'agents of social control' in the radical years.[12]

Riots and Tumults

Riots and disturbances were a feature of life in eighteenth-century Scotland, a troublesome feature for those in authority. Church patronage disputes were a common source of unrest and there were others. Opposition to customs and excise duties was one such popular cause. Christopher Whatley notes evidence from virtually every part of Lowland Scotland of disorder, mainly of assaults on customs and excise officers and attacks on their warehouses.[13] Excise duties levied on goods or commodities produced or sold within the country, such as malt, salt and soap, were particularly vexing as they hit the poor disproportionately hard. Other examples of the popular response to the harshness of life for those in humble circumstances were food riots and, in 1797, disturbances against the implementation of the Scottish Militia Act. In a study concentrating on Lowland urban society, Whatley discusses the authorities' fear of riots. The problem was all the more acute because of the lack of a police force. Troops sometimes had to be called out.

The great alarm which met an outbreak of food rioting in early 1720 on the east coast, from the vicinity of Edinburgh to Montrose, demonstrated the authorities' anxiety to avoid or dispel unrest. The riots of 1720 happened after a good harvest. However, exports commanded a premium and shortages were being experienced in the east-coast towns when shipments from the ports were all too evident. Food riots were normally avoided through paternalism. In this instance, the riots were a stern reminder to those in authority in Scotland of their paternalistic responsibilities and the consequences of forgetting them. Whatley observes how significant it was that grain and meal exports reached their peak for the century in the period 1717–22. After 1720 burgh councils and landed proprietors were sensitive to shortages and acted swiftly to deal with forestallers and to buy meal for distribution to the poor.[14]

The widespread militia riots of August and September 1797 were another case in point. English troops had to be brought in to help quell them. The most serious incident was at Tranent, where 11 people were killed when the Pembrokeshire Cavalry fired on the crowd. These riots were a reaction to the decision during the wartime emergency to raise a militia through compulsory service. This militia was to be used for peacekeeping and home defence, but rumours abounded that recruits would be sent overseas. The militia was to be drawn from the 19–23 year-old age group, selected through a ballot-based system. People of poor or modest means, the targeted groups, were acutely vulnerable to the loss of their breadwinners, hence the intensity of the disturbances. The authorities did not simply respond with repressive measures including the arrest of ringleaders, but defused things by taking popular anxieties on board. Upon receiving advice from Scotland, such as that from the deputy lord-lieutenant of Dumfriesshire, about the misapprehensions of 'the inhabitants' arising 'from a total ignorance of the Act and its intent', an educational campaign was mounted. The then home secretary, the Duke of Portland – who was on good terms with Henry Dundas and deferred to him in Scottish affairs – advised that notices should be put on church doors and that public meetings should be held to explain matters properly. There were also some local subscriptions by the gentry to fund substitutes for people who had been drawn in the ballot.[15]

Rioting was common in European countries, including England and Scotland. Historians consider, however, that Scotland was relatively quiet compared to others. That may be so. But the union with England added appreciably to the political impact of Scottish disturbances. At the union Scotland was already looked upon by England as a nuisance neighbour; and this attitude was strengthened when the Scottish Privy Council, which had jurisdiction in matters of riots, was abolished in 1708. Upon the demise of the Privy Council, the focus of concern at the centre of government on the problem of disturbances in Scotland moved to the office of whichever secretary of state in London was taking official responsibility for Scotland at the time (that is before the creation of the home office in 1782). A disagreeable lordly air towards Scotland may, at times, be espied in the correspondence of the non-Scottish secretaries. This was particularly true of the Duke of Newcastle's correspondence with the justice clerks, who reported to him from Scotland on such matters as 'disaffection' and unrest. Newcastle took on Scottish business from 1725 to 1742 and 1746 to 1754 as one of the secretaries of state. To Newcastle the problem was not *in* Scotland. It *was* Scotland. We may redress the balance a little by noting that the Scottish political manager in those days, Ilay (a person resented by Newcastle), was one of a small group of friends who surrounded Sir Robert Walpole, the prime minister, when the latter was jostled and insulted by an anti-excise mob in April 1733.

The suspicion held by some English politicians that the loyalty of those in authority in Scotland in dealing with social unrest was not to be assumed was epitomised by the severe reaction in Westminster to the lynching in 1736 of Captain Porteous of the Edinburgh town guard. Although political enemies of Walpole and Ilay worked up that reaction at Westminster to embarrass the prime minister and his Scottish manager Ilay (Chapter 4), there was a receptive audience at Westminster for those who demanded a severe response. Innate anti-Scottish prejudice was at work, but the Scots themselves were not always innocent. Above all, in 1725 the Duke of Roxburghe and his squadrone associate, the former lord advocate Robert Dundas, had, when Roxburghe was on the brink of losing office, encouraged the discontent that arose in Scotland when the malt tax was imposed. And there were common assumptions among politicians in England and Scotland that riots were inspired, managed or encouraged for political ends.

During the debate in the Scots parliament on the treaty of union, Daniel Defoe, Harley's informant in Edinburgh, had suspicions of that sort when he reported on the activities of the anti-union mob. The mob's activities including an attack on the house of Sir Patrick Johnston, one of the commissioners who negotiated the treaty. Defoe noticed that preceding the attack, when the city was in a 'most dreadful uproar and the High Street full of rabble', the Duke of Hamilton, who led the opposition to the treaty, came out of his lodgings and went up the High Street in his chair. Most people thought this was deliberately provocative, said Defoe. It 'was exactly calculated to begin the tumult, for the mob in a vast crowd attending him thither waited at the door – and as these people did not come there to be idle, the Duke could have done nothing more directly to point out their business, the late Lord Provost, Sir Patrick Johnstone, living just upon the spot.'

Some weeks before the union took place, Defoe reported on continuing unrest. He gave his own thoughts about the mob and its management: 'The mob are a machine; the Jacobites have wound them up to a pitch and nothing but time, management, temper and success can reduce them to the proper medium. They must be let run down gradually or they precipitate at once into all manner of confusion.'[16] At the other end of the century, the government, in their initial response to the militia riots, were no less sure that there were political forces involved. Convinced as usual that the 'emissaries of sedition' were at work, the authorities decided, explains E. W. McFarland, to detach and detain the leaders of the riots to, as it was put, 'undeceive the multitude and punish the seditious'.[17] Indeed, the extreme radical group, the United Scotsmen, did try to capitalise on the riots; but they were not the instigators. The radical challenge of the final years of the century was accompanied by mob activity, but was essentially more rational, although not recognised as such by the authorities. It attempted to base itself on reason.[18]

The Radical Challenge

The radical threat in Scotland peaked in 1792–93. As will be seen, however, even the first great symbol of the radical advance in Scotland, the formation of the Associated Friends of the People in July 1792, displayed signs of a movement that carried the seeds of its own destruction. Radicalism's peak, and its decline, in Scotland coincided with Henry Dundas's tenure as home secretary, 1791–94: in England its decline was discerned a little later. In Scotland Dundas met the challenge with the help of his nephew and son-in-law, Robert Dundas of Arniston, lord advocate, 1789–1801. As home secretary and one of the triumvirate heading the Pitt government, Henry Dundas was at the centre of the reaction to radicalism in England and in Scotland. Thus he pushed keenly for a royal proclamation to be issued against 'wicked and seditious writings'. This proclamation was designed, in part, to suppress Thomas Paine's *Rights of Man*. Following the issuing of the proclamation by Pitt in May 1792, Dundas championed a campaign to use the courts to attack sedition. And he was no less zealous, and successful, in fighting the radicals through intelligence gathering and harassment by *agents provocateurs*; through payments to newspapers and publishers; and through other forms of loyalist propaganda. In June 1792 Paine, who was then in England and had received a summons to answer charges, ended a letter to him with the words 'I am, Mr Dundas, Not your obedient humble servant, But the contrary.'[19] Paine fled to France in the following September.

In Scotland a more dramatic recognition of the home secretary's place in the competition between coercion and change was the hanging and burning of Dundas's effigy in some Scottish towns during riots in May and June 1792. Dundas visited Scotland as usual in the autumn, when parliament was not sitting. His stay was extended as he witnessed the growing menace of radicalism and unrest at first hand. He returned to London utterly determined to crack down on the democratic threat. In this, he reflected the general opinion of the enfranchised political nation in England and Scotland, including opposition reformist Whigs, at a time when matters were threatening to get out of hand.[20] Dundas was extraordinarily decisive and single-minded. In May he had written of taking such steps as should be thought necessary 'for repressing those pernicious practices and doctrines that are afloat and which cannot be met and resisted at too early a stage'.[21] To carry out this policy in Scotland, lord advocate Robert Dundas, who was also an MP, was given leave at the height of the threat to absent himself from parliament. It would be hard to demonise Robert. He was, said his cousin Lord Cockburn, 'a little, alert, handsome, gentleman-like man, with a countenance and air beaming with sprightliness and gaiety, and dignified by considerable fire; altogether inexpressibly pleasing.' Robert was Henry's trusted political factotum in Scotland.[22]

A variety of intellectual influences – ultimately the example of the French revolution and the publication of the *Rights of Man* – as well as the reactions of those in power and underlying changes in society, contributed to the radical threat of the 1790s and helped shape it. Before touching upon events in 1792–93, it will be helpful to mention some of the causes of the radicalism. It grew out of a combination of long-term developments and a more recent sequence of events. Perhaps most surprising at first glance are hints of a contribution from religious seceders to its growth. They were innately conservative and introspective in their religious practices, but were nurtured on anti-state prejudice. In McFarland's judgment, seceders seemed to be a significant presence in the ranks of the United Scotsmen – the secret organisation active in 1796–97, which had universal (male) suffrage as one of its objectives. The leader of the United Scotsmen, George Mealmaker, a weaver in Dundee, was a communicant of the Scottish relief synod. He was tried for sedition in January 1798 and sentenced to 14 years' transportation. McFarland traces his 'long and impressive pedigree' in Scottish radical politics. She reminds us that he wrote the Perth reformers' address, which resulted in September 1793 in the trial and transportation of the Reverend Thomas Fysche Palmer. Mealmaker, as secretary of the Dundee Friends of Liberty, had also been a delegate at the second national convention of the Scottish Friends of the People and at the third British convention and had been imprisoned in 1794.[23]

Also helping to foster radical ideas were attacks, stretching far back into the century, by opposition in parliament and 'out of doors', on a succession of ministries – attacks which labelled those in power as corrupt usurpers of traditional liberties. Among those who had articulated and popularised this opposition were Bolingbroke and Wilkes. The case of Wilkes shows how difficult it can be to measure such influences. His harping on in a Whiggish way about ancient liberties is said to have encouraged popular aspirations not just in England but in Scotland. Yet, it is hard to believe that his work, rich in anti-Scottish invective, could have had much of an educational impact in Scotland. There is rather less doubt that political sensibilities in Scotland were honed on the question of self-determination during the American War of Independence. Andrew Hook says, for example, that the treatment of the war in Scottish newspapers and magazines suggests a well-informed public; and that the Speculative Society in Edinburgh debated the controversy five times between 1768 and 1775. During the critical year 1776 – the year of the Declaration of Independence, in July – there was, in May, also considerable opposition among members of the popular party in the general assembly of the Church of Scotland to the government's American policies.[24]

Also relating to the American war and contributing to the Scottish nation's political education, was the movement which in 1778–82 rioted and declaimed successfully against relief for Catholics in Scotland. After a debate in the Commons on 14 May 1778 on a motion to give a measure of relief to English Catholics, Henry Dundas, who was then lord advocate, announced that a bill to give Scottish Catholics relief from the penal laws would be introduced in a later session. There was at that time an air of tolerance in parliament towards Catholics. To help recruit troops from Ireland and the Highlands, the government also had a strong incentive to remove bars against Catholics at a difficult stage in the war. The people who were visible to the historian as being active in the movement which forced the government to retreat from its plans for Catholic relief in Scotland, were 'otherwise worthy' working people from the middle and lower social classes, explains Robert Donovan, and they recruited others less fortunate than themselves. Their intolerant movement was in no sense radical. But it provided an education in popular protest. During and after the relief crisis, says Donovan, the experience of their campaign of 1778–82 encouraged a spirit of enquiry and protest, and organisation on issues beyond the 'sullen resentments' of anti-Catholicism. The campaign brought active and long-lasting political awareness to large numbers of people for the first time.[25]

In 1782 an intense, long-term campaign for Scottish burgh reform began. This campaign provided the Scots with a continuing political education. And the same classes of people and some of the leaders who joined in the pro-American and anti-Catholic causes supported it.[26] The thwarting of the burgh reformers' demands by Henry Dundas in parliament in April 1792 and the publication of the proclamation against seditious publications in the next month helped spark-off the disturbances and radical outburst of that year in Scotland. In dealing with the burgh reform movement, it is appropriate to refer to the economic and social background in which it and the later radicalism developed. The campaign for burgh reform began when there were moderate, and ultimately unsuccessful, pressures in England for parliamentary reform. However, the changes that had been taking place in Scottish society were a background circumstance of no less importance. Scotland was in a pre-industrial phase of economic development. There was long-term growth in commerce, population and the professional middle class, and accelerating movement into the towns. This was a fertile environment for frustration to develop with the way the 66 royal burghs, many of them petty communities, were governed. The burgh councils were seen as exclusive, self-electing, corrupt and inefficient oligarchies. In a report of 1789, the reformers gave examples of abuses or bad management by councils and, of course, dealt with the vital matter of self-election.

Dunfermline provided splendid evidence, including the case of John Wilson senior, who died in 1778: he 'had kept himself' on the council for almost 50 years, 'the greater part of which time', the report declared, he had the address to manage it 'in every political contest'. In Annan, it was said that: 'From about the year 1730 to 1762, the Borough was entirely under the management of Bryce Blair of Potterflatts, and his cousin John Johnston of Gutterbraes . . . who alternately, for two years, were Provosts of the Borough, and the Council was composed almost entirely of their relations. This duumvirate blew up upon Mr Blair's death in January 1762.' At that time: the members of the council were said to be Provost John Johnston, and the following members of his family: two sons, four nephews, one brother, one cousin and two sons-in-law. There were also instances of aristocratic influence in councils; such as in Dumbarton, where, said the report, there 'is a rigid adherence to the mandates of the family of Argyle, whose agent at this hour directs every circumstance relative to the annual elections within the Borough.' And there were non-resident councillors; such as in Whithorn where only five out of 18 councillors lived in the burgh, the rest (who paid no burgh taxes) living variously in Dumfries, London, France and in the countryside.[27]

After 1785 the campaign for burgh reform concentrated on remedying the corrupt system of administration in the burghs rather than confronting the system under which representatives were elected to parliament from Edinburgh and the ten districts of burghs. On the recommendation of the leader of the opposition Whigs in the Commons, Charles James Fox, the famous Richard Brinsley Sheridan, MP for Stafford, was appointed to champion the burgh reformers' cause in parliament. The leader of the opposition Whigs in Scotland, Dundas's old adversary Henry Erskine, dean of the Faculty of Advocates, was not an MP and there was almost no support for the cause among the Scots who were in parliament. Most of them were adherents of the administration. One of the members of the small Scottish opposition group, Lawrence Dundas's son, Sir Thomas Dundas, member for Stirlingshire, was chairman of the London Committee for Burgh Reform – but his zeal faded and he did not second Sheridan's parliamentary campaign in favour of reform in 1792. Sheridan himself was no match for Henry Dundas. The latter stifled the issue when it was raised by Sheridan in the House between 1787 and 1793.[28] The critical event in the Commons took place on 18 April 1792, when the House rejected Sheridan's motion for a committee of enquiry to be formed to look into maladministration in the burghs.

This rebuff was more than just another setback for the burgh reformers. It demonstrated the failure of their long-term campaign and provided them with an impetus to direct their energies towards wider reform. Popular discontent with the workings of the old system was all the more keen thanks to the inspiration of the French revolution and the *Rights of Man*; but these also implanted the seeds of the radical cause's failure. The violent progress of the revolution and Paine's extremism weakened the radical movement from within and encouraged the political establishment to unite to crush it. Events in France at the outset of the revolution were received with some enthusiasm and approval in the solid respectable core of society, as represented, for example, in the readership of the *Caledonian Mercury* and the *Edinburgh Gazetteer*, and among the Foxite, reformist Whigs who were in the minority in the political establishment. Popular enthusiasm was also fuelled by the *Rights of Man*. It was first published in two parts, in March 1791 and February 1792. A sixpenny edition followed. In November

1792 it was said that the book was 'being circulated throughout all Scotland, at a very low price' and that 10 000 copies a week were being sold.[29] Paine advocated political rights for all men, defended the French revolution and promoted the idea of the democratic republic. He was equally preoccupied with inequalities of wealth. His work was, in short, a threat to the existing order in Great Britain.

The establishment, the majority of the reformist Whigs included, was alarmed. And concern was heightened by the course of events in France. In August 1792 the French royal family was imprisoned. In September there were political massacres in Paris and the French republic was proclaimed. In January 1793 Louis XVI was executed. Not only did the British government react, but the Whig opposition – which had supported burgh reform over the years – began to temper its reformist zeal, such was the perceived threat to the status quo. In charting the rise and decline of the movement for parliamentary reform, John Brims points to the early loss of support for this radical cause in reformist opposition Whig circles. The majority of burgh reformers by nature were not themselves extreme radicals. So the leading reformist Whig, Henry Erskine, not only opposed parliamentary reform, he also worked hard in Scotland from April 1792 to warn the disappointed burgh reformers of the flame that would be ignited if they linked up with its supporters. In this he was largely successful.[30] The initial impetus among the burgh reformers to join the wider movement for constitutional reform weakened quickly. That weakness shaped the character of the Scottish Association of the Friends of the People from its foundation.

The Scottish Association's formation was preceded by the appearance of an association of 'societies of the friends of general reform'. This group, made up of people of relatively humble origin, was a modest enterprise with few members and little means. The Scottish Association was formed, at a meeting in Fortune's Tavern in Edinburgh in July 1792, when the Friends of General Reform met some dissident burgh reformers and Foxite Whigs who did not follow Erskine's advice on steering clear of the issue of parliamentary reform. The Scottish Association was, nevertheless, very sensitive to the danger of adopting parliamentary reform as an objective. In this, it followed the example of the English reformist Whigs who had formed the Association of Friends of the People in April 1792. The Scottish Association divorced itself from the Paineite doctrines, following its English counterpart in looking to constitutional means to effect its programme. Brims notes that the Fortune's Tavern meeting declared the Association's purpose as 'to take into consideration the means best adapted for restoring our constitution to its original purity'. The meeting resolved that the Friends of the People would 'attempt by all constitutional means' to secure 'an equal Representation of the People' and 'a more limited duration of Parliamentary Delegation'.[31]

It can be argued that there were two problems for the Friends of the People in this. First, in those stormy times – with the mob huzzahing for Paine and events about to turn particularly nasty in France – it was impossible for the Friends to satisfy the public mind that they would not inflame things and that their moderate constitutional intentions were genuine. Second, the declared objects of the Association contained contradictions that quickly undermined it. There was an appeal to Whig constitutionalism. Hence the conjuring up of the usual opposition Whig cant about returning the constitution to its (imaginary) original purity. The aim of limiting the duration of parliaments referred to another routine opposition call, to have elections more frequently than every seven years so as to make it more difficult, and costly, for those in power to use patronage and other bribery to manage parliamentary representation. The above aims of the Association were harmless enough. But the other aim, of securing an equal representation of the people, conflicted with the governing and propertied classes' belief in the relationship between liberty and the ownership of property.

The aim of equal representation was an extremely dangerous doctrine in those times. It could not possibly be achieved through constitutional means and made the association vulnerable to external attack and internal conflict, as well as weakening it through lack of support. The movement grew steadily at first and then spectacularly throughout Scotland between the meeting at Fortune's Tavern and December. However, the activities of the crowd and the happenings in France, assisted by government propaganda, led to alarm among the generality of the respectable and propertied classes, including those who did not have the vote. Backs were turned and faces were set against the Association. There was a campaign of repression including high-profile prosecutions and various forms of intimidation. The Association failed to convince that it was not behind the public unrest. Doubts began to set in within the Association itself. Brims observes how the inaugural meeting of the first national convention of the Scottish Friends of the People in December 1792 was dominated by loyalist reaction and a determination to 'maintain the established constitution of Great Britain', despite a strong level of support for radical policies.

There was little sign of any such radical policy in the movement's publications and utterances for the rest of the winter. The Foxite Whigs, in particular, were showing signs of cold feet and many withdrew their support when a second national convention was held in the spring. Moderatism again won the day at this convention, though there was a continuing determination to persevere with the cause of parliamentary reform by constitutional means. Support continued to dwindle in the early summer. A proposal, from Thomas Hardy of the London Corresponding Society, that the parliamentary reform societies throughout Great Britain should unite, raised flagging spirits and it was agreed to hold a British convention of the delegates of the people in Edinburgh in November 1793. A rump of extreme radical elements now prevailed. The mood of the third Scottish national convention was provocative. Matters at the following British convention got completely out of hand, with Jacobin forms of address being adopted and talk of 'the duty of resistance by force of arms'.

Brims's conclusion is that the destruction of the Scottish parliamentary reform movement was ensured by these 'mad proceedings'. In the midst of widespread public outrage, the *Caledonian Mercury* expressed the general satisfaction over the dispersal of the convention and the arrest of its leaders 'before the guillotine was declared permanent'. A few zealots limped on but the days of the Scottish radical reform movement were numbered.[32] The crushing of the English movement followed in early summer 1794. By this stage, the war with France (declared February 1793) dominated the government's thinking. The accusation against the radicals was now one of high treason rather than the lesser one of sedition, as had been the case in Scotland. It was believed by the government that the London radicals were, under direction from France, planning an armed rising in support of a French landing on the south coast.[33]

The radical threat sorely troubled the regime. John Burnett, who was one of the deputies to the lord advocate at the time, later wrote of 'the beginnings and progress of that innovating spirit, which at that period, had well nigh overthrown our constitutional establishments, as well as the vigour and efficacy of our Common Law, in repressing it'.[34] In retrospect, however, it is evident that the radicals did not have enough public support nor sufficient conviction for an extreme challenge to the existing order and that the government had the resources to defeat them. Contemporaries had different perceptions of the danger. Dundas used the resources of the state to deal with the threat. Strong though his reaction was, there was an underlying confidence that radicalism and revolutionary ideas were not the real challenge at the end of the century. Hence, in the war against revolutionary France, he was convinced that the real fight was in the colonies not in Europe. He held this view in 1795 just as he had done in 1793. His consistent theme was the protection and enlargement of Britain's commerce and national wealth, not fear of revolution.[35]

Postscript

Upon Pitt's resignation in 1801, the shock in Scotland was no less severe than it was in England. After his death in 1806, Pitt Clubs were formed in both countries to commemorate him as the great defender of the King and constitution. Scotland retained its own national and political concerns, but by the end of the eighteenth century, it was a strong partner in a changing British political world.

NOTES

Abbreviations

DNB	*Dictionary of National Biography*
HMC	Historical Manuscripts Commission
NAS	National Archives of Scotland (formerly the Scottish Record Office)
NLS	National Library of Scotland
PRO	Public Record Office
RSCHS	*Records of the Scottish Church History Society*
SHR	*Scottish Historical Review*

1   The Price of Scotland?

1. Sources used include the following. NLS: Darien Papers, in particular, Adv. MS. 83.2.4, List of proprietors and debts due to the company, 1707–9; Adv. MS. 83.1.7, Stock journal, 1696–1706; and Adv. MS. 83.5.2, Cash book, 1700–7. NAS: Records (incomplete) of the commissioners of the equivalent, E111, including records of certificates issued on the civil lists and the second general account. Royal Bank of Scotland Archives: Civil list certificates, among records of the equivalent. NAS: SP2/4/4–8, Warrant books of the secretary of Scotland, 1706–7.

2. P. W. J. Riley, *The English Ministers and Scotland, 1707–1727* (London, 1964), ch. 14.

3. George Lockhart, *Memoirs Concerning the affairs of Scotland from Queen Anne's Accession to the Throne to the Commencement of the Union of the Two Kingdoms of Scotland and England in May 1707* (London, 1714), p. 213.

4. NLS, Adv. MS. 83.2.4.

5. Margaret D. Young (ed.), *The Parliaments of Scotland: Burgh and Shire Commissioners* (2 vols, Edinburgh, 1992–93) is particularly valuable in providing biographical details.

6. NAS, Dunbar town council minute book, 1688–1715, B18/13/2.

7. The interest within a council of merchant and trade houses and craft incorporations who may have subscribed could also have influenced councils' intentions.

8. Peter C. Vasey, 'The Economy and Social Geography of Perth in the Late Seventeenth and Early Eighteenth Centuries'. unpubl. MSc thesis, Stirling University, 1987, p. 28.

9. Montrose District Archives, Brechin town council minutes, 1696–1707.
10. NAS, Hamilton Muniments, GD406/1/5487, 24 June 1707; GD406/1/ 7853, 2 September 1707.
11. Angus District Archives, Brechin council minutes.
12. Glasgow City Archives, Hammermen of Glasgow, minute book, 1616–1734, T-TH 2/1/1; collector's account book, 1691–1766, T-TH 2/2/1.
13. Glasgow City Archives, Coopers, collector's account book, 1686–1742, T-TH 10/4/1.
14. E. Beresford Chancellor, *The Lives of the Rakes*, vol. 3 (London, 1925); *DNB*, Francis Charteris.
15. Riley, *English Ministers*, p. 213.
16. Sir James Balfour Paul (ed.), *The Scots Peerage*, (Edinburgh, 1904–14), vol. VI, pp. 379–80.
17. There are a very small set of documents in the equivalent papers at the Royal Bank which refer to Queensberry's accounts and dues at the time of the union, but not to the £20 000. These may help resolve the questions relating to his finances. Among the large sums mentioned is £16 423 sterling from the customs of foreign excise at Glasgow and other Clyde ports as at Whitsunday 1704 (Ref. EQ/30/1).
18. P. W. J. Riley, *The Union of England and Scotland* (Manchester, 1978), pp. 256–9.
19. William Ferguson, *Scotland's Relations with England: a Survey to 1707* (Edinburgh, 1994), p. 266.

2   The Politics of Great Britain

1. NAS, Montrose Muniments, GD220/6/1778, anon., 1708.
2. Romney Sedgwick (ed.), *Letters from George III to Lord Bute, 1756–1766* (London, 1939), pp. xi–v.
3. Brian Hill, *The Early Parties and Politics in Britain, 1688–1832* (Basingstoke, 1996), p. 28.
4. Daniel Szechi, (ed.), *Letters of George Lockhart of Carnwath, 1698–1732* (Edinburgh, 1989), p. xiv.
5. Jennifer Mori, *William Pitt and the French Revolution, 1785–1795* (Edinburgh, 1997), p. 12.
6. See Mark Goldie (ed.), *Locke: Political Essays* (Cambridge, 1997), p. xxv.
7. Frank O'Gorman, *The Long Eighteenth Century: British political and social history, 1688–1832* (London, 1997), pp. 44–5, 142–5.
8. J. M. Gray (ed.), *Memoirs of the Life of Sir John Clerk . . . Extracted by Himself from His Own Journals, 1676–1755* (Edinburgh, 1892), p. 47.
9. Henry St John, *Viscount Bolingbroke, A Dissertation upon Parties: in Several Letters to Caleb D'Anvers Esq.* (10th edn, London, 1775), pp. 2–3.
10. P. W. J. Riley, 'The structure of Scottish politics and the Union of 1707', in T. I. Rae (ed.), *The Union of 1707: Its Impact on Scotland* (Glasgow, 1974), pp. 7, 11; William Ferguson, *Scotland 1689 to the Present* (Edinburgh, 1968), p. 137.
11. David Hayton, 'Traces of Party Politics in Early Eighteenth-Century Scottish Elections', in Clyve Jones (ed.), *The Scots and Parliament* (Edinburgh, 1996).

12. Szechi, *Letters of George Lockhart*, pp. 136–7. The interpretation is Szechi's.
13. HMC, *The Manuscripts of His Grace the Duke of Portland Preserved at Welbeck Abbey*, (vols III–V, London, 1894–99), vol. IV, p. 560.
14. Hill, *Early Parties and Politics in Britain*, pp. 146–7.
15. David J. Brown, 'The Government of Scotland under Henry Dundas and William Pitt', *History*, 41 (1998), p. 271.
16. O'Gorman, *The Long Eighteenth Century*, p. 201.
17. NAS, Montrose, GD220/6/1971/1.
18. Jeremy Black, *Robert Walpole and the Nature of Politics in Early-Eighteenth-Century England* (Basingstoke, 1990), p. 108.
19. Mark A Thomson, *The Secretaries of State, 1681–1782* (repr., London, 1968), pp. 31–2, 147, 164–6.
20. See John Dwyer and Alexander Murdoch, 'Paradigms and Politics: Manners, Morals and the Rise of Henry Dundas, 1770–1784', in John Dwyer et al. (eds.), *New Perspectives on the Politics and Culture of Early Modern Scotland* (Edinburgh, 1982), pp. 217–20, which explains the exodus differently.
21. Michael W. McCahill, 'The Scottish Peerage and House of Lords in the late eighteenth century', *SHR*, 51 (1972), p. 186.
22. T. M. Devine, *The Transformation of Rural Scotland: Social Change and Agrarian Economy, 1660–1815* (Edinburgh, 1994), pp. 45–7.
23. HMC, *Portland*, V, p. 313.
24. I am obliged to Dr. David Hayton for this information.
25. Dwyer and Murdoch, 'Paradigms and Politics', p. 214.
26. R. G. Thorne, *The History of Parliament. The House of Commons, 1790–1820* (London, 1986), vol. I, p. 73.
27. David J. Brown, 'Henry Dundas and the Government of Scotland', unpubl. PhD thesis, Edinburgh University, 1989, pp. 107–13; Sir Lewis Namier and John Brooke, *The History of Parliament. The House of Commons, 1754–1790* (London, 1964), p. 480; Brown, 'The Government of Scotland', p. 271.
28. Bedfordshire County Record Office, Lady Lucas' Collection, Wrest Letters, L30/9/17/15x, Breadalbane to the Marchioness Grey.
29. Michael Fry, *The Dundas Despotism* (Edinburgh, 1992), p. 88.
30. David J. Brown, '"Nothing but Strugalls and Coruption": The Commons' Elections for Scotland in 1774', in Jones, *The Scots and Parliament*, p. 101.
31. David J. Brown, Thesis, p. vi.
32. An incomparable work in tracing the social and political integration and success of the Scots is Linda Colley's *Britons: Forging the Nation 1707–1837* (London, 1992).

3 The Struggle for Control, 1707–25

1. David Hayton, 'Constitutional experiments and political expediency, 1689–1725', in Steven G. Ellis and Sarah Barber (eds), *Conquest and Union: fashioning a British state, 1485–1725* (Harlow, 1995), p. 302.

2. Ronald Sunter, *Patronage and Politics in Scotland, 1707–1832* (Edinburgh, 1986), pp. 78–9, 199–210.
3. NAS, Montrose, GD220/5/795–7.
4. Ibid., GD220/5/797/1.
5. Alexander Cunningham, *The History of Great Britain: from the Revolution in 1688 to the Accession of George the First*. Translated from the Latin with an introduction by William Thomson (2 vols, London, 1789), vol. II, pp. 270–2.
6. Riley, *English Ministers*, p. 110.
7. NAS, Montrose, GD220/6/1778.
8. Ibid., GD220/5/177/1, 12 June 1708.
9. Gray (ed.), *Memoirs*, pp. 71–2.
10. George Macaulay Trevelyan, *England under Queen Anne* (3 vols, London, 1931-4), vol. III, p. 58.
11. Riley, *English Ministers*, pp. 246–7.
12. Edward Gregg, 'The Jacobite Career of John, Earl of Mar', in Eveline Cruickshanks (ed.), *Ideology and Conspiracy: Aspects of Jacobitism, 1689–1759* (Edinburgh, 1982), p. 180.
13. HMC, *Portland*, IV, pp. 630, 633.
14. Ibid., V, pp. 303–4.
15. Ibid., p. 243.
16. Ibid., p. 312.
17. Ibid., p. 100.
18. NAS, Montrose, GD220/5/808/10.
19. Bedford County Record Office, Wynne MSS, WY897-900, Letter books of the Duke of Argyll, 1711–12. Letter to Queen, n.d., in WY897.
20. Riley, *English Ministers*, p. 242.
21. HMC, *Report on the Laing Manuscripts Preserved in the University of Edinburgh*, vol. II (London, 1925), p. 169.
22. Trevelyan, *England under Queen Anne*, vol. III, p. 242.
23. Ragnhild Hatton, *George I: Elector and King* (London, 1978), pp. 108–9, 335. Hatton's source is Henry L. Snyder, 'The Last Days of Queen Anne. The Account of Sir John Evelyn examined', in *Huntington Library Quarterly*, 1971.
24. HMC, *Fifth Report*, (London, 1876), p. 618.
25. HMC, *The Manuscripts of the Duke of Athole and the Earl of Home* (London, 1891), p. 66.
26. Hatton, *George I*, pp. 125–6.
27. NAS, Montrose, GD220/5/340/3, GD220/5/429/4–5; *Culloden Papers* (London, 1815), p. 34.
28. Correspondence in NAS, Montrose, GD220/5/440.
29. NAS, Montrose, GD220/5/590/1.
30. Charles Sanford Terry (ed.), *The Chevalier de St George and the Jacobite Movements in his Favour* (London, 1901), p. 305.
31. *Culloden Papers*, p. 62.
32. William Coxe, *Memoirs of the Life and Administration of Sir Robert Walpole, Earl of Orford* (3 vols, London, 1798-1816), vol. II, p. 61; Hatton, *George I*, pp. 198–9.

33. See *DNB*, Charles Spencer, third Earl of Sunderland.
34. Coxe, *Walpole*, vol. II, pp. 60–78, 144–6, 158–62.
35. Romney Sedgwick, *The History of Parliament. The House of Commons, 1715–1754* (London, 1970), vol. I, pp. 26–7, 83; Riley, *English Ministers*, pp. 267–8.
36. Hatton, *George I*, pp. 245–6.
37. NAS, Montrose, GD220/5/828/12; NAS, Stair Muniments, GD135/141/19A.
38. HMC, *Polwarth*, III, p. 249.
39. Ibid., pp. 248–9.

4 From Ilay to Dundas

1. Barbara L. H. Horn, 'Domestic Life of a Duke: Cosmo George, Third Duke of Gordon', unpubl. PhD thesis, Edinburgh University, 1977, pp. 246, 565.
2. NAS, Irvine Robertson Papers, GD1/53/95/11, anon., [*c.* 1745].
3. Szechi, *Letters of George Lockhart*, pp. 130–1.
4. On the Great Marlborough Street properties, see *Survey of London*, vol. XXXI (London, 1963), pp. 251–262, 289–301. On Kenwood, see Julius Bryant, *The Iveagh Bequest: Kenwood* (London, 1995), pp. 58–9.
5. *Survey of London*, vol. XXXI, p. 295.
6. NLS, Saltoun Papers, MS 16591, ff. 53–6.
7. Robert Halsband (ed.), *The Complete Letters of Lady Mary Wortley Montagu* (Oxford, 1965–67), vol. III, pp. 97, 176.
8. Mavis Batey et al., *Arcadian Thames: the river landscape from Hampton to Kew* (London, 1994), pp. 64, 77.
9. James A. Home (ed.), *Lady Louisa Stuart: Selections from her Manuscripts* (Edinburgh, 1899), p. 14.
10. NLS, Saltoun, MS 16552, ff. 107–9.
11. Sedgwick, *The House of Commons, 1715–1754*, vol. II, pp. 446–7.
12. NLS, Saltoun, MS 16591, ff. 125–6.
13. John, Lord Hervey, *Some Materials towards Memoirs of the Reign of King George II*, ed. Romney Sedgwick (3 vols, London, 1931), vol. I, pp. 44–5, vol. II, pp. 139–40.
14. O'Gorman, *The Long Eighteenth Century*, p. 74.
15. Alexander Murdoch, *The People Above: Politics and Administration in Mid-Eighteenth-Century Scotland* (Edinburgh, 1980), p. 32.
16. Hervey, *Memoirs*, vol. II, pp. 660–1.
17. Richard Scott, 'The Politics and Administration of Scotland, 1725–1748', unpubl. PhD thesis, Edinburgh University, 1981, pp. 442–4.
18. Sedgwick, *House of Commons, 1715–1754*, vol. I, pp. 46–7.
19. NLS, Saltoun, MS 16587, 18 Feb. 1742.
20. Duncan Warrand (ed.), *More Culloden Papers*, (Inverness, 1923–29), vol. V, p. 36.
21. Scott, Thesis, pp. 514–5.
22. Ibid., pp. 516–7, 522.
23. Murdoch,*The People Above*, pp. 40–53.
24. Ibid., pp. 44–7. See also the important work of John M. Simpson, 'Who

Steered the Gravy Train, 1707–1766?', in N. T. Phillipson and Rosalind Mitchison (eds), *Scotland in the Age of Improvement* (Edinburgh, 1970), p. 62. Simpson's understanding of Duke Archibald's role as political manager is unsurpassed.
25. Ibid., pp. 50–1; E. M. Lloyd, 'The Raising of the Highland Regiments in 1757', *English Historical Review*, 17 (1902).
26. Roger L. Emerson, 'Lord Bute and the Scottish universities 1760–1792', in Karl W. Schweizer (ed.), *Lord Bute: Essays in Re-interpretation* (Leicester, 1988).
27. Alexander Murdoch, 'Lord Bute, James Stuart Mackenzie and the government of Scotland', in Schweizer, *Lord Bute*, p. 125.
28. See Linda Colley's analysis of the Wilkes phenomenon in *Britons*, pp. 105–17.
29. See Stanley Ayling, *George III*, (London, 1972), pp. 70–1.
30. John Ehrman, *The Younger Pitt: the Consuming Struggle* (London, 1996), p. 423.
31. Stephen Wood, *The Scottish Soldier* (Manchester, 1987), p. 37; Colley, *Britons*, pp. 126–8; Ayling, *George III*, p. 103.
32. Wood, *The Scottish Soldier*, p. 38.
33. Of particular value to me have been the recent work of David Brown on Dundas's Scottish politics and the assessment by Michael Fry in *The Dundas Despotism* of Dundas's role in promoting the British 'Empire of trade'.
34. Brown, 'The Government of Scotland', pp. 275–7.
35. Brown, '"Nothing but Strugalls and Coruption"', pp. 103–5.
36. Brown, Thesis, pp. 39–40, 45; 'The Government of Scotland', p. 267.
37. Ehrman, *The Consuming Struggle*, p. 380.
38. Brown, 'The Government of Scotland', p. 269.
39. Paul Kelly, 'British Parliamentary Politics, 1784–1786', *The Historical Journal*, 17 (1974), pp. 738–42; Brown, 'The Government of Scotland', p. 270.
40. Brown, 'The Government of Scotland', pp. 272–3.
41. Donald E. Ginter (ed.), *Whig Organization in the General Election of 1790: Selections from the Blair Adam Papers* (Berkeley, California, 1967), p. xxxiv.

5   The Jacobites

1. See H. T. Dickinson, 'The Jacobite Challenge', in Michael Lynch (ed.), *Jacobitism and the '45* (London, 1995), p. 7.
2. Allan Macinnes, *Clanship, Commerce and the House of Stuart, 1603–1788* (East Linton, 1996), p. 181.
3. Eveline Cruickshanks and Jeremy Black (eds), *The Jacobite Challenge* (Edinburgh, 1988), p. 4.
4. Jeremy Black, *Culloden and the '45* (Stroud, 1990), pp. 63–5.
5. Edward Gregg, 'The Politics of Paranoia', in Cruickshanks and Black, *The Jacobite Challenge*, p. 42.
6. Bruce Lenman, *The Jacobite Risings in Britain 1689–1746* (London, 1980), pp. 222–3.
7. *Clanship, Commerce and the House of Stuart*, pp. 169–77, 180–1.

8. Murray G. H. Pittock, *The Myth of the Jacobite Clans* (Edinburgh, 1995), p. 46; 'Who were the Jacobites?', in Lynch, *Jacobitism and the '45*, pp. 60, 65–8.
9. *The Myth of the Jacobite Clans* , pp. 99–100.
10. Tristram Clarke, 'The Williamite Episcopalians and the Glorious Revolution in Scotland', *RSCHS*, 24 (1990), pp. 48–50.
11. For the details of the employment and offices open to them, I rely on Paul Kléber Monod, *Jacobitism and the English People, 1688–1788* (Cambridge, 1993), pp. 280–2, Eveline Cruickshanks, *Political Untouchables: the Tories and the '45* (New York, 1979), p. 4, and on the Acts of parliament cited.
12. Monod, *Jacobitism and the English People,* pp. 146–63.

6   The Leadership's Ideas and Aspirations

1. NAS, Montrose, GD220/6/504/3, 7.
2. Andrew S. Skinner, 'Pufendorf, Hutcheson and Adam Smith: Some Principles of Political Economy', *Scottish Journal of Political Economy*, 42 (1995), p. 169.
3. NLS, Saltoun, MS.16529, 6 Feb. 1724. The catalogue of his library was published as *Catalogus Librorum A.C.D.A.* (Glasgow, 1758).
4. Richard Scott, Thesis, p. 358.
5. Brown, Thesis, p. 94; Piers Mackesy, *Statesmen at War: the strategy of overthrow, 1798–1799* (London, 1974), p. 5.
6. Mackesy, *Statesmen at War*, p. 11.
7. Scott, Thesis, p. 358.
8. NAS, Montrose, GD220/5/838/18; Szechi, *Letters of George Lockhart*, p. 178. Graham Townend, 'The Scottish Nobility and the House of Lords, 1715–1722', in *Power, Property and Privilege. The Landed Elite in Scotland from c.1440 to 1914*, Association of Scottish Historical Studies (St Andrews, 1989), p. 44.
9. Brown, Thesis, p. vi.
10. Richard Saville, *Bank of Scotland, A History, 1695–1995* (Edinburgh, 1996), p. 175.
11. Christopher A. Whatley, *The Industrial Revolution in Scotland* (Cambridge, 1997), p. 13.
12. O'Gorman, *The Long Eighteenth Century*, pp. 135–6. Jeremy Black, *The Politics of Britain, 1688–1800* (Manchester, 1993), p. 77.
13. Kelly, 'British Parliamentary Politics, 1784–1786', p. 753.
14. Murdoch, *People Above*, p. 127; Murdoch, 'The Importance of Being Edinburgh: Management and Opposition in Edinburgh Politics, 1746–1748', *SHR*, 62 (1983), pp. 5–6.
15. T. M. Devine, 'The American War of Independence and Scottish Economic History', in Owen Dudley Edwards and George Shepperson (eds), *Scotland, Europe and the American Revolution* (Edinburgh, 1976).
16. Michael Duffy, *Soldiers, Sugar, and Seapower* (Oxford, 1987), pp. 7–14.
17. I am very grateful to William Bigwood for this information on the fisheries.
18. *Industrial Revolution in Scotland*, pp. 41, 46.

19. See NLS, Culloden Papers, MS.2967, f. 3, 29 Jan. 1726.
20. Robert Wodrow, *Analecta*, ([Edinburgh], 1842–43), vol. IV, p. 191.
21. *Bank of Scotland*, pp. 54–6.
22. Coutts & Co. Archives, Letter book 14, 1 Oct. 1720.
23. These matters are dealt with in expert detail in Saville, *Bank of Scotland*, chs 4–6. See also Shaw, *Management of Scottish Society*, pp. 118–24, 130–2.
24. *Bank of Scotland*, pp. 173–5.
25. Charles Sanford Terry (ed.), *The Albemarle Papers* (Aberdeen, 1902), vol. II, p. 479, letter to Newcastle, Dec. 1747.
26. T. C. Smout, 'Where had the Scottish economy got to by the third quarter of the eighteenth century?', in Istvan Hont and Michael Ignatieff (eds), *Wealth and Virtue: The Shaping of Political Economy in the Scottish Enlightenment* (Cambridge, 1983), p. 69.
27. NLS, Saltoun, MS.17594, ff. 5–10, copy letter to Mr Goodchild.
28. John Robertson, *The Scottish Enlightenment and the Militia Issue* (Edinburgh, 1985), pp. 9–11, 15–16, 22–38.
29. Ibid., p. 147.
30. Fry, *The Dundas Despotism*, p. 219.
31. Piers Mackesy, *War without Victory: the Downfall of Pitt* (Oxford, 1984), pp. 11–14, 80–93, 98.

7   Reaction and Radicalism

1. Roxburghe Papers, bundle 726, 18 Apr. 1725.
2. Lionel K. J. Glassey, 'William II and the Settlement of Religion in Scotland, 1688–1689', *RSCHS*, 23 (1989), pp. 323–6.
3. Goldie, *Locke: Political Essays*, p. xxiv.
4. Quoted by Shaw, *Management of Scottish Society*, p. 99.
5. PRO, State Papers Scotland, Church Book 1742–64, SP56/2, pp. 10–11.
6. Shaw, *Management of Scottish Society*, p. 104.
7. Henry Sefton, 'Rev. Robert Wallace: An Early Moderate', *RSCHS*, 16 (1966), pp. 1–22, 'Lord Ilay and Patrick Cuming: A Study in Eighteenth-Century Ecclesiastical Management', *RSCHS*, 19 (1977), pp. 203–16; J. Warrick, *The Moderators of the Church of Scotland, 1690–1740*.
8. Dr Laurence Whitley's generosity in giving me papers on the years after the revolution is greatly appreciated. The few points I mention can only give a poor reflection of his work.
9. Sefton, 'Robert Wallace', p. 9.
10. Sefton, 'Lord Ilay and Patrick Cuming', pp. 203–4.
11. I am grateful to Dr David Brown for this point.
12. Richard Sher and Alexander Murdoch, 'Patronage and Party in the Church of Scotland, 1750–1800', in Norman Macdougall (ed.), *Church, Politics and Society: Scotland, 1408–1929* (Edinburgh, 1983); Brown, Thesis, pp. 391–2, 397.
13. 'How tame were the Scottish Lowlanders during the Eighteenth Century?', in T. M. Devine (ed.), *Conflict and Stability in Scottish Society, 1700–1850* (Edinburgh, 1990), p. 7.
14. Ibid., p. 17.

15. E. W. McFarland, *Ireland and Scotland in the Age of Revolution: Planting the Green Bough* (Edinburgh, 1994), pp. 163–5.
16. HMC, *Portland*, IV, pp. 340, 390.
17. McFarland, *Ireland and Scotland in the Age of Revolution*, p. 165.
18. See Stana Nenadic, 'Political Reform and the "Ordering" of Middle-Class Protest', in Devine, *Conflict and Stability*.
19. John Keane, *Tom Paine: A Political Life* (London, 1995), p. 341.
20. John Brims, 'The Scottish Association of the Friends of the People', in Devine, *Conflict and Stability*, pp. 37–40.
21. Holden Furber, *Henry Dundas, First Viscount Melville, 1742–1811* (Oxford, 1931), p. 79.
22. Thorne, *The House of Commons, 1790–1820*, vol. III, p. 646.
23. McFarland, *Ireland and Scotland in the Age of Revolution*, pp. 156, 160–1; John Burnett, *A Treatise on Various Branches of the Criminal Law of Scotland* (Edinburgh, 1811), pp. 258–60.
24. Andrew Hook, *Scotland and America: A Study in Cultural Relations, 1750–1835* (Glasgow, 1975), pp. 64–7.
25. Robert Kent Donovan, *No Popery and Radicalism: Opposition to Roman Catholic Relief in Scotland, 1778–1782* (London, 1987), pp. xiii, 7–8, 121, 147.
26. Ibid., p. 307.
27. NAS, Irvine Robertson, GD1/53/102. Substance of the Reports of Grievances Transmitted by the Committees of Burgesses of Different Boroughs, in Answer to the General Instructions Transmitted by the Committee of Convention at Edinburgh, March 31, 1789. Printed.
28. Thorne, *The House of Commons, 1790–1820*, vol. I, pp. 78–9.
29. Keane, *Tom Paine*, p. 331.
30. 'The Scottish Association of the Friends of the People', p. 33.
31. Ibid., pp. 32–5.
32. Ibid., pp. 33–45.
33. Mori, *William Pitt and the French Revolution*, p. 192.
34. Burnett, *Criminal Law of Scotland*, p. 241.
35. See, for example, Mori, *William Pitt and the French Revolution*, pp. 156–7, 212–3.

INDEX

A

Abercrombie, Alexander, of
  Glasshaugh, 14
Aberdeen, William Gordon, second
  Earl of, 95–6
Aberdeen burghs, 70
Aberdeenshire, 33
Act of Settlement (1701), 1
Adam, William, MP, 37, 82
Adderbury, Oxfordshire, 66
Addington administration, 79
Addison, Joseph, 44
African Company, *see* Darien
  Company
Alien Act (1705), 1
Alston, Rev. James, 111–12
Alves, William, writer in
  Edinburgh, 5
America, 35, 74, 98–9, 123
  Declaration of Independence, 122
  War of Independence, 79, 80, 98–9,
    106, 122
  East and West Florida, 78
  Locke's *The Fundamental
    Constitutions of Carolina* (1669),
    110
Anglesey, Arthur Annesley, fifth Earl
  of, 52
Annan, burgh of, 123
Annandale, William Johnstone, first
  Marquis of, 13, 40
Anne, Queen, 23, 25, 28, 40, 41, 42,
  46, 48, 52, 53, 60
annexed estates commission, 87, 97,
  103–4
Argyll, Archibald, ninth Earl of,
  40
Argyll, Archibald Campbell, first
  Duke of, 41, 65

Argyll, Archibald Campbell, Earl of
  Ilay, third Duke of, 15, 28
  background and education, 30, 63–
    5, 66–7, 94
  relations with his brother, 34, 47,
    67, 70–1
  politics of, 24–5, 51–2
  Harley (Lord Oxford) and, 46, 48–52
  political frustrations of, 29, 30, 37,
    46, 50–4, 65, 66, 67–8
  anti-union calls and, 52–3, 56
  lord justice general, 54, 58, 64
  squadrone and, 31, 38, 40–3, 49
  Junto and, 31, 38, 42–3
  Marlborough, the Marlborough
    clique and, 38, 42–3, 50, 60, 69
  during the '15, 56–8
  Whig schism and, 58–60
  comes into favour, 59–62
  Walpole and, 58-62, 67, 68, 70, 74,
    118, 119
  political manager, 33–5, 37, 48–50,
    57, 64, 68–71, 72–4, 95, 97, 100,
    103, 110–12, 113, 115–16: *see
    also* Milton, Andrew Fletcher,
    Lord
  political monopolist, 63–4, 101
  political skills of, 39, 55–6, 61, 74
  Porteous affair and, 69–70
  attitude to church, 110–11, 113–16
  Duke of Newcastle, 34–5, 36,
    68, 72–4, 118
  George II and, 26, 36, 67–8: as
    Prince of Wales, 58
  Henrietta Howard and, 67–8, 101
  Jacobites and, 31, 84, 87, 90
  Duke of Cumberland and, 36, 72,
    73
  Carteret and, 70, 71
  Henry Pelham and, 25, 72–3

Argyll, Archibald Campbell, Earl of
Ilay, third Duke of *continued*
Henry Fox and, 74
raising of troops and, 74
Lord Bute and, 74–6
his life in London and Twickenham,
64–7
enthusiasms of, 25, 64–7, 94–6
interest in banking and speculation,
93, 100–2
economic improvement and, 55,
87–8, 93, 97, 103
Argyll, Archibald Campbell, Marquis,
41, 115
Argyll, Archibald Campbell, ninth
Earl of, 40
Argyll, Elizabeth Tollemache, Duchess
of, 41, 54, 65
Argyll, John Campbell, second Duke
of, 10, 96
promotes union of 1707, 15, 18
childhood, 65
military career, 30–1, 42, 47, 56–8,
71
in London society, 30, 63, 65–6
relations with his brother, 34, 47,
67, 70–1
Whig credentials of, 24–5; and
politics of, 26, 29, 34, 47–8, 51–
2, 53, 54, 70–1, 95
Tories and, 43, 48, 58
attitude to church, 114–15
personality, 25, 26, 39, 41, 46, 47,
52, 63–4, 65, 71
political interest at a low ebb after
union, 39
squadrone and, 31, 38, 40–3, 55–6
Junto and, 31, 38, 42–3
Marlborough, the Marlborough
clique and, 38, 42–3, 47–8, 50,
57, 58, 60, 61
Harley (Lord Oxford) and, 46, 48–
52
political frustrations of, 46, 50–5,
58–9, 65, 67–8, 71
anti-union calls and, 52–3, 56
the defence of the Hanoverian
succession, 54, 56
the '15 and, 56–8
Whig schism and, 58–60
George II and, 26, 67–8: as Prince
of Wales, 54, 58–9
return to favour, 59–62

Earl and Duke of Greenwich, 15, 47,
51, 60–1
political interest of, 5, 39, 40–1, 43,
48, 51, 101
political monopolist, 63–4
banking and finance and, 101–2
Walpole and, 34, 58–62, 68, 70–1,
75
Porteous affair and, 70
Lord Bute and, 74–5
Argyll, John Campbell, fourth Duke
of, 64
Argyll estates, 64, 65
Argyll family, 68, 123
Argyllshire, 41, 88
army, 11–12, 36, 42, 46–47, 52, 54,
56–8, 71, 72, 74, 78–9, 91, 98,
102, 117, 122
Atholl, John Murray, first Duke of, 10,
13, 50, 54
Atterbury plot, 86
Augusta, dowager Princess of Wales, 75
Ayr burghs, 75
Ayrshire, 41, 70

B

Baillie, George, of Jerviswood, 28, 61
Banffshire, 33
Bank of Scotland, 96, 101, 102–3
Bennet, Sir William, of Grubbet, 108
Blair, Bryce, of Potterflatts, 123
Bland, Humphrey, 87, 103
board of control, 80, 82, 95
board of trustees for fisheries and
manufactures, 87–8, 93, 97, 100
Bolingbroke, Henry St John, first
Viscount,
career in government, 48–9, 52, 53
ambitions towards Scotland, 49
Jacobite associations, 51, 69, 86, 87
in opposition to Walpole, 69, 122
political writing, 20, 22–3, 69, 74,
76, 122
Boyle, Henry, secretary of state, 48
Breadalbane, John Campbell, third
Earl of, 33–4
Brechin, 6–7, 8–9
British Linen Company, 93, 103, 104–
6
British Museum, 66
Buccleuch, Henry Scott, third Duke
of, 29, 80, 103

Loudoun, Hugh Campbell, third Earl
of, 27, 40

M

Macgregor, Rob Roy, 41
Mackenzie, James Stuart, 27, 28, 75,
76
Mackenzie, Roderick, of Prestonhall,
5
magnates, influence of, 5–6, 23–4, 26,
29, 31, 48–9, 64, 73, 123
Maitland, John, Duke of Lauderdale,
65
Malplaquet, battle of, 46–7
malt tax, 52–3, 61–2, 100
Mandeville, Bernard, 105
Mansfield, William Murray, first Earl
of, 36, 78, 95
Mar, John Erskine, Earl of, 16, 39, 44
secretary of state: Scottish, 27;
British, 27, 28, 49, 51–2, 54, 56
client and friend of Lord Oxford, 49
election manager for Oxford, 49–51
relations with Argyll and Ilay, 49–
50, 52
Jacobitism of, 46, 51, 56–7, 87
1715, 56–7
Marble Hill, Twickenham, 67
Marchmont, Alexander Hume, second
Earl of, 102
Marchmont, Patrick Hume, first Earl
of, 5, 42
Marchmont family, 31, 40
Marlborough, John Churchill, first
Duke of, 46, 54
duumvir in power with Godolphin,
42
enemy of Argyll and Ilay, 38, 42, 50,
57, 58
Argyll seeks his downfall, 47, 50
his clique, 42, 58, 61, 69 : its links
with the Junto and the
squadrone, 42–3, 61
Marlborough, Sarah Jennings,
Duchess of, 46
Mealmaker, George, 121
Melfort, John Drummond, Earl of,
86–7
Melrose, Coldstream and Binning,
lordship of, 16
Melville, Andrew, reformer, 110

Melville, George Melville, Earl of,
113–14
Middleton, Charles Middleton,
second Earl of, 86–7
Middleton, George, goldsmith, the
Strand, 101–2
Middleton, Colonel John, 56
militia issue, 105–6
Milton, Andrew Fletcher, Lord, 64,
67, 103
Ilay's (third Duke of Argyll's)
manager in Scotland, 33, 34, 71,
72
management of the church, 110,
111–12, 115–16
lord justice clerk, 64: his use of the
position, 72
and the squadrone, 31, 71–2
and Jacobites, 72
befriends the military, 72, 87, 103
Cumberland's opinion of, 72
the board of trustees for
manufactures, 87–8, 100
the annexed estates commission, 87,
103
views on Highland society, 87, 103–
4
the British Linen Company, 93,
104–5, 106
promotes the value of self-interest,
104–5, 106
works with James Stuart Mackenzie,
76
Minch, the, 99
Mississippi scheme, 101
Mitchell, Sir Andrew, 31
Mitchell, Rev. William, 115
moderate literati, 106
Mollison, Francis, Brechin, 7
Montagu, Lady Mary Wortley, 66
Montrose, James Graham, first Duke
of, 13, 26, 43, 60, 69, 94
rewarded at the union, 15
background, 24, 40, 63, 94
a leader of the squadrone, 26, 40
misplaced hopes in 1708 general
election, 45
purchase of Lennox estates in 1704,
40–1
territorial and political rivalry with
Argyll, 40–1
associations with Glasgow and
Dunbartonshire, 40–1, 94